Breakthrough
COACHING

Breakthrough
COACHING

Creating
Lightbulb Moments
in Your Coaching
Conversations

Marcia Reynolds

BK
Berrett–Koehler Publishers, Inc.

Berrett-Koehler Publishers, Inc.
1333 Broadway, Suite 1000
Oakland, CA 94612-1921
Tel: (510) 817-2277
Fax: (510) 817-2278
www.bkconnection.com

ORDERING INFORMATION
Quantity sales. Special discounts are available on quantity purchases by corporations, associations, and others. For details, contact the Special Sales Department at the Berrett-Koehler address above.
Individual sales. Berrett-Koehler publications are available through most bookstores. They can also be ordered directly from Berrett-Koehler: Tel: (800) 929-2929; Fax: (802) 864-7626; www.bkconnection.com.
Orders for college textbook / course adoption use. Please contact Berrett-Koehler: Tel: (800) 929-2929; Fax: (802) 864-7626.

Distributed to the U.S. trade and internationally by Penguin Random House Publisher Services.

Berrett-Koehler and the BK logo are registered trademarks of Berrett-Koehler Publishers, Inc.

Printed in Canada

Berrett-Koehler books are printed on long-lasting acid-free paper. When it is available, we choose paper that has been manufactured by environmentally responsible processes. These may include using trees grown in sustainable forests, incorporating recycled paper, minimizing chlorine in bleaching, or recycling the energy produced at the paper mill.

Library of Congress Cataloging-in-Publication Data
Names: Reynolds, Marcia, author.
Title: Breakthrough coaching : creating lightbulb moments in your coaching
    conversations / Marcia Reynolds.
Description: First edition. | Oakland, CA : Berrett-Koehler Publishers,
    Inc., [2024] | Includes bibliographical references and index.
Identifiers: LCCN 2023030370 (print) | LCCN 2023030371 (ebook) | ISBN
    9781523004829 (paperback) | ISBN 9781523004836 (pdf) | ISBN
    9781523004843 (epub)
Subjects: LCSH: Personal coaching. | Executive coaching. | Counselor and
    client.
Classification: LCC BF637.P36 R489 2024 (print) | LCC BF637.P36 (ebook) |
    DDC 158.3—dc23/eng/20231020
LC record available at https://lccn.loc.gov/2023030370
LC ebook record available at https://lccn.loc.gov/2023030371

First Edition
31 30 29 28 27 26 25 24   10 9 8 7 6 5 4 3 2 1

Book producer: PeopleSpeak
Text designer: Reider Books
Cover designer: Adrian Morgan

For the thousands of coaches around the world
who are passionate about the difference we make
to inspire positive action and uplift the human spirit.
Please take my work as an expression of my
gratitude for your bravery and commitment.

I also dedicate this work to my coach trainer
colleagues, especially those who operate coaching
schools in countries facing chaos, both economically
and politically, where actions have cost many lives.
I am honored to teach by your side as we confirm our
beliefs in the transformational powers of coaching.

Contents

PART TWO:
Maintaining a Client-Centered Focus

PART THREE:
What Is Their Desired Outcome *Really*?

PART FOUR:
Debugging the Operating System

PART FIVE:
Turning Insights into Commitments

The Science of Learning and the Role of the Coach

Thirty-five years ago, I enrolled in my second master's degree in adult learning psychology. I had been teaching leadership and communication skills classes for two companies I worked for. People liked the classes; they gave me happy faces on my evaluation forms. Then they went back to doing what they had always done before the class.

I wasn't changing minds. People I taught may have learned facts, formulas, and good reasons for changing, but they did not make permanent leaps in their behavior.

I was hoping the graduate studies would lead me to the secret to changing people's minds and behavior. I learned a lot, but not the secret.

For years after I graduated, I continued to take workshops and read books to increase the impact of my teaching. I saw improvement, but I felt more disappointed than fulfilled.

I decided to do my own informal research. Each day, I sat with someone new at lunch in the cafeteria. I found both former class participants and managers who had sent their people to my classes. I shared my observations and asked what value they thought my training provided.

I concluded most people were not committed to permanently changing their behavior. They committed to trying new behaviors, but the shift back to doing what they had always done before came quickly. They reported small wins, such as having more patience with others and courage to speak up more often with peers and in meetings. When it came to bigger changes, they said they didn't have time to practice.

After further investigation, I determined that as soon as new behaviors felt awkward and they were afraid of being judged by others, most people reverted back to their safe behaviors, even when they knew they weren't getting the best results from their workplace interactions.

I didn't lose hope. There had to be something I could do that would motivate people to commit to growing even when it felt awkward or scary. I continued my research and attended workshops as often as possible to make my training programs better. Then something happened that interrupted and redirected my search.

In October 1995, I resigned from the third company I worked for. That day, a friend sent me an article she had read in *Newsweek* about this new phenomenon springing up in the United States called *coaching*.

The article mentioned a coaching school. I called and after watching a coaching demonstration, I enrolled. I knew I had found what I had yearned for. The shift in the feelings of the person being coached was palpable. The client went from confusion and frustration to excitement and gratitude. When she stated what she was going to do next, her conviction was solid. Because she was a classmate in the coaching school, I was able to follow her growth. The shift she made in that session changed the view she had of herself as well as of her challenge. She never went back to her old self. Coaching had changed her life.

I had witnessed a learning technology that generated long-term behavioral change.

Not long after, I read Daniel Goleman's book *Emotional Intelligence*. I realized how important emotional states and reactions were to sustainable growth and how this was only a minor consideration in my education. I looked deeper into the new avenues of neuroscience that were emerging since the invention of the fMRI made it possible to track and measure brain activity. I created a training program for using emotional intelligence in leadership conversations and was quickly asked to teach my program around the world. The excitement generated in these classes prompted me to learn more.

My discoveries led me to finding a doctoral program that would support my research in neuroactivity related to learning. I realized coaching enhanced awareness, solution recognition, and commitment to act through insight creation in accessing the regions of the brain associated with creativity. I have been adapting and strengthening my coaching and training approaches ever since I was introduced to this new profession. I am passionate about continually discovering and sharing ways we work with people to learn and grow.

Why We All Need a Coach to Grow

I learned from the first management training program I taught that you can't tell people to change and expect them to comply. Everyone seems to know this, but knowing doesn't stop them from doing. Think of the times you tell others what to do because you think you are helping or saving time. As a teacher, I fall into this trap as well. If I am the wise elder they came to for enlightenment, why would I engage them in an interactive conversation where I would spend most of my time listening? Telling people what to do is a routine habit easily rationalized.

Unless someone begs you for direction and suggestions, you are wasting time dispensing wisdom.

From my research and experiences, I now know the reason why people persist in doing what they have always done no matter how good the trainer or book is because the brain would rather keep you in your comfort zone than take risks. The brain prefers to conjure rationalizations for repeating behavior instead of seeking reasons to continuously grow.

> People safely live inside old stories based on past experiences because their brains prefer self-preservation over self-actualization.

Even when you attempt change, you rarely give up how you did things before. Carin Eriksson Lindvall, head of the Unit for Career and Leadership at Uppsala University in Sweden, said humans don't change habits and behaviors even when they have experienced undesirable results; most routines are never questioned. You may try to solve a problem by adding a suggested behavior, but when the change feels frustrating or awkward, you'll most likely go back to old routines, which take less brain power. She said, "By definition, routines are solutions to yesterday's problems, and they are freeing. They relieve us of having to think through every step we take."[1]

The brain doesn't like to work too hard, especially when the outcome is uncertain. Family therapist Virginia Satir reportedly said, "People prefer the certainty of misery to the misery of uncertainty." When you don't have any past experiences indicating how to succeed in the present situation, the brain defaults to predicting failure. The fight-or-flight response kicks in, prompting you to resist or avoid taking the risks required to grow.

You have an operating system running continuously in the background of your brain throughout the day, so you rarely stop to deeply consider what you should do next. It relies on the past to give meaning to the moment (reality) and how you define yourself in relation to what you see (identity). It activates repeated patterns of behavior, including how to react to uncertainty.

Psychologist Dan McAdams of Northwestern University equated life narratives to personal myths.[2] Although your stories do not support your best interest or unspoken desires when faced with current situations, he says these narratives provide a sense of consistency. Old goals, obsolete values, and outdated self-perception are the "core planks of a life narrative" that give you a false sense of security. The brain dodges the state of *not knowing* with convenient rationalizations. Yet accepting not knowing is an essential step to opening to what else is possible to move life forward. You have to quit knowing to start growing.

Often you will live by *shoulds* that keep you from what you most desire. *Shoulds* come from what we think our family, friends, managers, or society want us to do. *Shoulds* sometimes provide moral direction. Other times, blindly obeying *shoulds* makes us feel unfulfilled, irritated, or empty.

> Most of us numbly spend our days repeating routines and behaviors without question. We live by the constructs and rules that have hardened over time.

You can't count on your brain to make the best decisions or help you understand what is causing your confusion when trying to sort your thoughts on your own. Self-reflection can lead to choosing an option for action, but you most likely will not go beyond the boundaries of the stories holding your perception of reality and identity in place.

How Coaching Overrules
the Protective Brain

Even when you know how your brain might keep you from acting in your best interest, it is difficult to coach yourself and nearly impossible if you have any emotions attached to the issue. Your brain will fool you into thinking you are objectively thinking when you aren't even close. Mark Leary said in his article "The Case For Being Skeptical of Yourself," "The real world and our interpretations of it are fused so tightly that we rarely realize how deeply our perceptions of reality are tainted by our beliefs, self-views, perspectives, and life experiences."[3] No matter how much you want something, you can't separate your brain's current version of reality from what else is possible.

To see the world and yourself differently, you need help extracting the stories defining your perspective to examine and change them if needed. You can't do this on your own; your attempts at objective contemplation trigger your brain to resist what feels uncomfortable. Neuroscientist Michael Gazzaniga said we get stuck in our automatic thought-processing and fool ourselves into thinking we are acting consciously and willfully.[4] You then stay safe—and stuck.

Gazzaniga also said that if you have an *external thought disruptor*—someone who reflects your words, expressed emotions, contradictions, and what seems to be the source of your hesitations—you can detach and view your stories as if they were a movie to be observed and analyzed. An external thought disrupter doesn't tell you to think differently. The disruption comes from concise reflective statements and curious questions that stimulate you to examine the thinking patterns and frameworks directing your decisions, overriding the protective brain. The insights you gain from external thought disruption disrupt your brain's operating system, allowing you to consciously and willfully decide what is best for you right now.

A good coach is a skillful thought disrupter. Using a respectful coaching approach breaks through the frames of your stories. Your perspective of yourself and the dilemma you are experiencing expands. Options appear. The choice you have been wanting to make all along shines through. Instead of feeling you will come out as a loser if you give up your beliefs, you see what's in it for you to gain.

Educational reformer John Dewey said, "Provoking people to think about their thinking is the single most powerful antidote to erroneous beliefs and autopilot."[5] Reality is persistent, but when a coach breaks through the frames of your stories, the emerging insights expand what is possible, affecting your decisions, actions, and life.

Dewey also said the most intelligent people need the most help thinking about their thinking. Smart people are the best rationalizers. They believe their reasoning wholeheartedly and will protect their opinions as solid facts. Telling them to change is a waste of time. Using strong reflections and questions is the only way to get smart people to question their thoughts.

Creating Breakthrough Moments Using a Coaching Approach

You don't have to be a trained coach to use a coaching approach that breaks through someone's automatic rationalizing and imaginary outcomes. If you feel compassionately curious with a sincere desire to understand how a person thinks, your presence soothes their fear of judgment. They sense you are there for their higher good and may feel safe enough to respond to the reflections you share and the questions you ask. If they have moments of hesitation or resistance, and you don't negatively react to their emotions, their mental fog will clear enough to see a step they can take toward achieving their desired outcome.

Even if you simply summarize their spoken thoughts and then ask questions about what their words mean, they may begin to wonder why they think the way they do. Maintaining your presence and curiosity is more important than trying to be profound. Your caring curiosity provides the safety they need to explore how their words represent their thoughts with you.

Their insights may trigger an emotional response. The first time a person sees with unfiltered clarity how their behavior and decisions have impacted their life can be an unpleasant and upsetting experience. A painful realization is a healthy part of the process.

You may have heard of the saying "No pain, no gain" when it comes to physical training. The saying can also be applied to mental growth. Discomfort is evidence that a new awareness is forming.

When you give people a moment to process what they now see with kindhearted silence, their emotional reaction will subside. When you sense they are settling down, you can ask them if they would share what they now see. Painful, embarrassing, and heart-wrenching realizations may be inevitable, but with coaching, most people feel lighter and optimistic after experiencing a lightbulb moment and talking through what the new awareness means to them.

When you refrain from judging or trying to fix people when they are emotionally processing their new way of seeing, they see beyond their stories, their limiting beliefs, and the conflicts created by their *shoulds*, opening to what else is possible to think and do. When they articulate the insight they had and what action they will take next, you have facilitated the breakthrough process. As they see themselves and their situations in a new light, they not only feel more confident to implement decisions and actions but also they are excited to take risks and move forward.

This *Breakthrough Coaching* book provides the essential skills for using reflective inquiry supported by resources and exercises so you can open people's minds and transform their thinking in a way that they can't do in self-reflection. Shifts are made in both identity and reality. This process ensures long-term change both in perception and action. With active support over time, the new ways of thinking and behaving become the typical way of doing things, at least until the next breakthrough experience.

The Breakthrough Coaching Program

The book complements the coach training program I deliver online for Coaching.com, formally known as the World Business & Executive Coach Summit. I delivered my first breakthrough coaching program in 2020. To my delight, over 27,500 people registered to watch my masterclass promoting the program, with nearly 14,000 showing up in person, and many more watched the recording. I am humbled, grateful, and sincerely convinced of the power of coaching to transform minds, hearts, and actions.

The breakthrough coaching program is now in a self-study format, so people around the world can access the material at any time of day, as many times as they desire. The program is supported by a live global learning community where coaches gather to do exercises, practice coaching, and discuss what they are learning. I do live Q & A sessions and coaching demonstrations in support of the programs as well.

What's next? That's the question the coaches frequently ask. We are offering an advanced Breakthrough Coaching program starting in 2024 to provide advanced coach training and the opportunity to practice the exercises suggested in this book plus two or three additional exercises aligned with each chapter. More information can be found at the end of this book.

My intention is to offer books and programs in support of your ongoing learning while on the journey of mastery in coaching. The five parts in this book cover the essential skills:

Part 1: How to Embody a Coaching Mindset
Part 2: Maintaining a Client-Centered Focus
Part 3: What Is Their Desired Outcome *Really*?
Part 4: Debugging the Operating System
Part 5: Turning Insights into Commitments

Each part has chapters with supportive resources and a practice exercise to help you integrate your learning. The resources and exercises are provided to give you a guide to discuss and try out new ways of coaching with others. It is a book you do, not just read.

Why I Developed This Program

I wrote my last two books, *The Discomfort Zone* and *Coach the Person, Not the Problem,* to fill in the knowledge gaps I saw in some coaches whom I worked with worldwide. Over the years, I noticed coaches trying too hard to demonstrate each competency no matter the coaching situation. The harder they worked, the less effective they were. Their attempts to do perfect coaching made them feel more stressed and frustrated. They were stuck in their heads, not being present and listening for the key words and moments that, when reflected back to the client, could cause the shift in perspective that changed minds and possibly lives.

The coaches were also taught misinterpretations of the coaching competencies that limited their abilities. Most were not taught how best to use closed questions, how to address the social needs and conflicts of values restricting growth, and how to effectively use reflections without questions to provoke creative insights. Coaching felt more formulaic than spontaneous. Coaches were not fully open and ready to receive whatever was presented. Key moments were missed. Critical but understated pieces of the puzzle were bypassed.

I came to coaching as a part of my incessant desire to understand what makes people learn and grow. Once I discovered the difference in impact of coaching from teaching, advising, mentoring, and counseling, I devoted my learning to discover how best to use the specific technology of coaching to transform minds and choices.

As I learn from my research and practice, I share what I am discovering in my writing, classes, and, most significantly, coaching demonstrations I do monthly so people can see what I teach. The reactions are the same wherever I go: "Thank you for liberating me from the rules I thought I had to follow." Coaches tell me they better understand the unique gift coaching provides.

Breakthrough Coaching includes the new teaching, exercises, examples, and tools that I developed since writing *Coach the Person, Not the Problem*, with at least 80 percent of the material being new. The book is intended to be a companion guide to my training as well as a stand-alone book for people to dive deeper into using a coaching approach in their conversations.

Coaching can be easy. The easier it is, the more meaningful and joyful the practice becomes.

My Passion for Coaching

I am doing what I can to help open minds and strengthen human connections. When people stay stuck in their old stories, they live more in fear than fulfillment. This creates conflicts and separation. I believe a coaching approach in our conversations can make our lives and relationships feel more rewarding and enjoyable.

The vision at Coaching.com is to radically shift the global professional coaching industry toward excellence by continually providing coaches with more knowledge and skills. The founder, Ben Croft, said, "Together, we passionately believe by empowering coaches through deeper learning, we can help change the world." I fully embody this philosophy.

When people know and feel their highest and most powerful self, they are often inspired to help others feel the same. *Breakthrough Coaching* can uplift and positively energize people around the world even when darkness tries to crush hope. Will you join me in this movement?

PART ONE

How to Embody a Coaching Mindset

The willingness of someone to engage with you as a coach depends on the energetic connection you create with them through your feelings, beliefs, and full-bodied attention. The practice of being fully present with an open mind and compassionate heart starts with yourself. You develop awareness of your emotions, beliefs, and needs so you can move them out of the way when coaching. Your presence creates a safe container for coaching. Your presence also affects what you hear, see, and receive as your coachee relives their experience with you.

The energetic connection is dependent on how safe the coachee feels with you. The strongest predictor that people will connect and open up to you is when you accept and respect who they are and what they say. They feel safe when they know you won't judge what they say and that you will appreciate their perspective no matter how different it is from your own. They feel valued as well as seen.

Six studies, and many that have followed, provided evidence that sincere respect is the strongest stimulus of positive feelings when interacting.[1] When it comes to creating trust and safety, feeling respected beats out the other factors, including compassion. They will feel safe enough to trust you when they feel that your intention is for their gain and your belief in their ability to grow is genuine.

Do you care about what is important to them? Do you believe in their abilities even more than they do? Can you maintain your sense of their intrinsic value throughout the conversation? You are answering yes to these questions when you demonstrate your belief that the person you are coaching is smart enough to discover solutions without you telling them what to do. You have no doubt they are fully functional, not inadequate and in need of your advice. You hold their dreams and desires as important even if you want something else for them.

Presence is not an action but a positive dynamic state of energy that forms and maintains the connection between you and the person you are coaching throughout the conversations. They feel you care and are there for their growth from the moment they see you in the room or online. Your presence will open or close the door to their acceptance of how you use your skills.

CHAPTER 1

What It Means to Embody a Coaching Mindset

W hen you first learn to coach, you practice applying the core competencies. Then you must trust that you know what to do, forgetting the specifics of the requirements. You coach by heart, not from your head. You get better at this with practice while knowing improvement is a continuous journey.

You must let go of being the perfect coach. Your clients need you to be present more than they need you to ask the perfect question. You don't have to coach flawlessly to receive and offer back what you think was expressed. When you are wrong and they correct you, you both better understand their thinking. When you trust that you will make a difference for them by creating a safe space to talk while using reflective inquiry as best you can in the moment, you are a good coach.

There is a commonly held idea that you need ten thousand hours of practice to be a master.[1] This belief suggests that mastering a skill has an end point. Whether this is true for some skills, in coaching, mastery is an ongoing journey. Deliberate practice makes you better at applying your skills, but how you continually deepen your full-body presence while performing creates the profound results you seek. There is not a path *to* mastery but a path *of* mastery.

You develop your mastery as you feel comfortable enough with your skills to let go and ride the ebb and flow of the conversation, receiving and offering back what seems to be the most meaningful elements in what the person shares with you. You receive their words, expressions, and energetic shifts. You offer what you experienced for them to consider. They will have emotional reactions as they examine the construction of their stories, deconstructing what doesn't serve them and considering new ideas as they come to light. If you stay with them throughout the process, not worrying about the mechanics of your practice, the session will be successful.

They may not have a clear aha moment with you, but they will continue to think about the conversation; the lightbulb may come on in the days that follow. The creative insights that emerge in the moment and over time are the measures of success in coaching.

French philosopher Simon Weil said, "Attention consists of suspending our thought, leaving it detached: empty, and ready to be penetrated . . . waiting, not seeking anything, but ready to receive."[2] Presence then calls on you to release the chatter in your mind to be open to receive what you hear, see, and sense from the people you are with.

You receive what they offer with no judgment. You trust what you offer back for them to consider is worthwhile. When you are curious, caring, and respectful, you are embodying a coaching mindset.

Do You Want to Be Proficient or Profound?

Even when you know how important it is to cultivate a coaching mindset, the increasing obsession of coaches intent on meeting certification requirements or safely following a coaching model undermines this development. Both leaders and coaches I work with find it difficult giving up a trusted script of standard questions and leading coachees to the conclusion they know is best. They miss the magic of being fully with the person in their conversations.

I support the development of skills and expertise. I teach coaching skills and mastering the competencies as defined by the International Coaching Federation (ICF) to coaches and leaders worldwide. Every class I teach includes structural elements of the conversation, but I also emphasize the importance of feeling humble and nonjudgmental while my students apply their technical skills.

It can take months, maybe years, to maintain being fully and sincerely present while developing your conversational competencies. Working on peeling away the grasp of your ego—the practice of *unselfing*—must be woven into your regular practice. This is your path to mastery.

> To be of value to your clients and colleagues, you must seek to be profound with your presence as well as proficient with your skills.

You must trust that whatever level of skill you have right now is enough, knowing breakthroughs can happen anytime you pull yourself out of the interaction. Your focus should never be on what *you think* about what they share. Your responsibility is to coach them on what *they think* about what they share with you when you coach them to see their thoughts more broadly, clearly, and objectively.

Practice Unselfing

To expand the awareness of others through coaching, you must release your concept of self. The identity you hold on to today brought you to your current comfort level no matter your level of self-worth. Giving up the value you believe you can provide for others as you have done in the past is not easy. Listening to someone speak without wanting to shape what will transpire takes courage.

Philosopher and novelist Iris Murdoch said that to experience beauty, we must learn the process of "unselfing."[3] Although she writes about unselfing when we commune with nature and contemplate art, I believe you can unself when you sense the sacredness of the human you are with. You release the worry that your value will be judged, freeing yourself of the clutches of your ego. Murdoch said, "Any real understanding of goodness is necessarily an embrace of imperfection." Only then can you attend to the phenomenon appearing outside yourself.

To unself while coaching, you must believe the energy that connects, aligns, and fosters insights to surface is more powerful when you are not analyzing or considering what to say next. You trust in the magic of the coaching process.

For example, being proficient at the ICF competency of setting an agreement for the conversation means you and your coachees become clear about what they want to have at the end of the conversation. They may say they want to make a decision, determine steps to take, or gain more clarity on their options. Go further. Wonder what it looks like when they make the decision, what they dearly want to create when they take the steps, or what truly is important to them about their desire to choose right now. Don't use your memory to ask a list of generic questions. Use their words as you explore what they hope for could look like and what making this picture real would mean to them.

Then keep wondering. Sense what they want that they have resisted saying or even formulating. Hear the angst in their words when they describe how they feel slighted by others, what they fear they have lost for good, and what they doubt they can do.

You respect their reactions and accept their grievances as data that will help you both define what is possible to create instead of suffering with what they have now. This will bring them to voice the real outcome they want to achieve.

Unselfing is clearly a good idea but difficult to do. Applying your coaching skills while being present will take patience as you are overcoming a lifetime of distracting mental habits. You must be courageous; standing in the present without thinking can feel unnerving. It can also be magical as you discover you are wiser and more capable than you ever imagined. I have learned that the less I say, the more profound I am. You will be amazed with not only the contentment you feel when you work in the present but also the positive results that show up.

When you observe with an accepting and caring mindset, you will not only be a masterful coach, but you will also have a greater appreciation of life. Take a moment before every conversation you have to consider how you can release your thoughts to witness the awesome uniqueness of the person you are about to engage.

When we unself, we free ourselves of identity, feel the sacredness of the journey, and lose ourselves to the alchemy. There is no anxiety from detaching, no fear of rejection and no need for a satisfying result.

BREAKTHROUGH COACHING RESOURCE

Unselfing—Becoming Profoundly Present

Self-transformation means we cross over (*trans*) so something new emerges (*formation*) in our sense of who we think we are. We must let go of something to give space for what is new. The process of releasing and recognizing is experienced by both you and the client as together you nurture deeper understanding and realizations that light a new way forward.

In order for the client to feel you are there for them and you won't judge their words or reactions, you must unself by releasing these five mental habits:

1. Needing for the client to find the session valuable
2. Knowing where the conversation will or should go
3. Dwelling in the client's story and pain
4. Wanting to be appreciated
5. Clinging to being the expert, leader, mentor, problem-solver, or parent

These habits come from wanting to feel good about who you are as their coach. They are fueled by the fears of rejection and insignificance. They block connections and the possibility of transformation.

The collective mind can emerge when the coach releases needs, opinions, and awareness of what is best to happen next. The coach must remain calm and comfortable to sense the experience with the client. Then information can flow into the coach, and the coach can offer it back impartially for clarification and understanding. The spontaneous loop expands thinking. Consciousness lifts for both the coach and client.

Coaching feels easy and graceful when letting the mind run freely in the open, unselfed field. The coach's presence is strong yet subtle; it is greater than one's self but doesn't reduce the self.

It is helpful to develop new mental habits that support unselfing throughout each day. Then before engaging in a coaching conversation, practice the following steps:

1. *Open yourself to being a self-less witness*—Walk inside or out for ten to fifteen minutes with a quiet mind. Notice your world without your *I* getting in the way—what you think about what you see. Instead, just notice your experience. What makes you smile, feel curious, or open with gratitude? What colors and details pop out? What are you seeing that you didn't see the last time you walked in this space? We miss so much when the *I* that defines our self leads us through life. If thoughts enter your mind, notice if there is anything important to consider, and then let them float away, knowing you can come back to them later. Release your *I* so you can be with the world around you.

2. *Bring your self-less witness into the conversation*—Sit comfortably in a chair, exhale fully, and feel your body relaxed but awake. You feel energy moving up and down the center of your body from your gut to the top of your head, simultaneously calming your body while sparking your curiosity. Your entire presence is attuned with this moment.

3. *Envision your client as strong, complete, and capable of achieving great things*—Your belief that the client is resourceful

and not broken or inadequate will raise the level of energy between you, even if they start the conversation doubting themselves.

4. *Let courage and love fill your body with warmth*—Remember you are a compassionate thinking partner. Your courage will inspire their willingness. Your care and belief in them will activate their confidence. The way forward will emerge as you knew it would all along.

CHAPTER 2

Aligning Your Nervous System

P sychological safety—the belief that one can speak up without risk of punishment or humiliation—has become a buzzword in the corporate world. Yes, it is a critical driver of a healthy, engaged workplace and innovative decision-making, but it is often written on walls as a corporate value yet forgotten under pressure.

Amy Edmondson, a Harvard business professor, said, "Psychological safety describes the individuals' perceptions about the consequences of interpersonal risks . . . how others will respond when one puts oneself on the line, such as by asking a question, seeking feedback, reporting a mistake, or proposing a new idea."[1]

Safety is a reaction, not a calculation. The brain stops people from speaking what is on their minds if they see any indication—real or not—that they will be embarrassed or hurt by your words. This automatic response happens before logic can assess the situation.

Creating a safe and supportive coaching relationship goes beyond your promise of confidentiality and telling them they have nothing to fear. Most people have been judged, embarrassed, or retaliated against many times in their lives. As adults, they resist intimacy. Their protective armor is readily available if not already covering their heart.

Never assume enough safety is present to establish trust. You need to consciously engender safety by feeling open throughout your body and being willing to receive whatever they offer before you start the conversation. The energy you physically create will either develop or detract from the safety others feel when with you.

When researching my book *The Discomfort Zone*, I discovered the importance of opening the three major organs connected by the vagus nerve that make up the nervous system when working through a difficult conversation. I found that using curiosity to open the mind, love and respect to open the heart, and courage to open the gut would deepen our ability to hear, sense, and ask about what others were experiencing.

I didn't know then that simultaneously opening the head, heart, and gut would deepen the feeling of safety others would have, even when the conversation was uncomfortable. I was teaching a workshop in Canada when a colleague handed me the therapeutic presence research of Shari Geller and Stephen Porges.[2] Their study found trauma patients felt safe enough for the first time in their lives to speak of a past trauma when the therapist visualized and used emotions to open their own head, heart, and gut before the therapy session.

I have since worked with coaches to open their head, heart, and gut using exercises such as the one shared at the end of part 1 to both create psychological safety and receive what is being expressed even beyond the spoken word. They go beyond cognitive awareness to using sensory awareness to gather the data they need while clients feel safe enough to share what they may not have even admitted to themselves before. Then the acceptance and appreciation of what they express solidifies their feelings of safety and trust.

Cognitive versus Sensory Awareness

You likely spend most of your time using your cognitive awareness. You seek to understand situations and people by interpreting what you see and hear. You might think you have empathy because you assume you know what they are thinking. The trap of cognitive empathy is your belief that you have also lived through their experience, which is not possible because your perspective is influenced by your past that is unique to you.[3]

When you coach using only cognitive awareness, you may revert to the habit of thinking about your thinking, where you are analyzing and evaluating your own thoughts instead of just receiving what you hear and see and offering it back for their reflection. Relying on cognitive awareness inhibits your data gathering; you may miss key details that indicate what is behind their fears and limiting perceptions. Also, if they sense you are critically analyzing what they say, they might feel a break in the energetic connection you had developed and less safe to tell you what is actually going on for them.

You must have sensory awareness as well as cognitive awareness to be able to fully receive the experience of the person. Sensory awareness includes an inward awareness of your reactions in a conversation. You instantly sense when your body tightens up, choking off your presence. As you develop the habit of quickly catching and relaxing any time a point in your body tenses up, you not only maintain safety in your conversations but also are more open to sense what they are experiencing as they talk.

You might sense fear, sadness, or disappointment. Because you must process what you sense in your brain to translate the sensation into language, your interpretation is biased by your past experiences. That is why you offer what you hear, see, or intuit from your heart and gut as an invitation to consider, not as a fact. You might say, "It seems to me there is some fear, sadness, or disappointment. What do you think about this, or is there something else?" The invitation is for them to confirm, modify, or correct what you share.

Start with "When you talked about _____ (using their words), it seems to me there was _____." You could be wrong; even being wrong can deepen their thinking and understanding. Breakthroughs often happen when your assessment is wrong!

The more you blend cognitive with sensory awareness, the better your results. Lean into your heart and gut more often. They have so much to tell you that you often don't hear.

What It Feels Like to Open Your Nervous System

You were likely taught to cut off from your senses as a part of your conditioning as a child. Were you ever told, "You shouldn't take things so personally" or "You're too soft. You should toughen up"?

You learned to block people from getting under your skin. You disconnected from them and yourself.

I'm often asked if venturing into the land of emotions is risky, especially at work. People always told me, "I can't show I'm emotionally affected by what is going on, and I certainly can't allow people's emotions to sway me." The business world is full of aphorisms that declare "Only the tough survive."

In the context of coaching, being sensitive is a strength, not a weakness. When you open yourself to feel your client's experience, you not only better receive meaning from them, but you also create the energetic environment that encourages them to feel safe enough to open to you.

When you listen only from your head, you focus on problem-solving instead of getting beneath the surface to discover what needs to be addressed that is making it difficult for the coachee to solve the problem on their own. Often when you think about only what they are saying, you tend to move the conversation quickly toward goals. You might hear and ask about a belief that could be holding them back or an assumption about the future that feels like a risk too scary to take, which is still good coaching but will only ensure incremental change at best.

When you listen with your body, opening your full self to the conversation, the results can lead to revolutionary change because you are receiving so much more information and insight to consider. You slow down the conversation knowing that the true desired outcome—what the person actually wants to do or be—comes from the exploration that leads to a broader awareness of how they see themselves and what is possible in the future. You listen with both a curious mind and open, compassionate heart to share and ask about what they are struggling to face. You will sense what they need to let go of to take the brave step to achieving what they want for themselves.

The conversation may feel uncomfortable for both of you. When you fully open your nervous system, you are sitting in your most vulnerable state. If they discount what you offer or react harshly, you may feel hurt more deeply than when your brain is prepared to defend you.

You have to trust that the process is working and stay open no matter how they react. When you crack through the walls around their stories, they might get angry, embarrassed, or sad. They might cry or lash out at you as a last ditch effort to protect themselves from the new picture of reality that is coming into view.

Stay courageously calm and compassionately curious. It is up to you to release your discomfort so you can coach people through theirs.

Accessing Your Head, Heart, and Gut Brains

Your head brain identifies cognitive formations—how the other person reasons, analyzes, synthesizes, and makes meaning of what is perceived. You use your head brain to recognize the assumptions and beliefs they are relying on to define their story. You hear the ratio-nalizations they are using for justifying their decisions and actions. They often are not aware of the reasons for their words. Hearing their not-so-logical reasoning played back to them can open the door to considering other viable options.

Your heart brain senses relational desires and influences—love and fear, hurt and resentment, belonging and rejection, disappoint-ment and submission, and hope and grief. When receiving communi-cation from this center, you can feel the energy found in the emotional texture of the person's words when they feel yearning and doubt, the sadness from loss of dreams, and the hesitation stemming from guilt. Their expression often shifts when they longingly state what they want and then quickly add the words "but" or "I should," which often indicate fear of failure or the need of approval from others.

Your coaching might focus on confirming what they said they wanted and then following with why they can't have it. You might hear what they are afraid to lose if they act differently, overshadowing what they can gain or what they will regret not doing in the future. You might explore identities they are holding on to from the past when their definition of self must change to move forward. You want to coach them to speak of dreams they haven't shared and what is possible today and in the next few years. Eventually, they will release the hold their fears have on their hopes.

Your gut brain reacts to impulses of self-preservation—the impulse to act based on anger or frustration. From this center, you sense what they have not declared that is keeping them from making a decision or moving forward. When their story keeps going in cir-cles or they insist the change is too hard to make, mobilize your own courage to explore what you feel they are clinging to and not wanting to let go of to move on. The loss they are afraid of facing could be anything from a job title or role, a friendship, or their self-worth.

What will it take to let go, and who will they be when they do? Acknowledge the normality of their fears and confusion while challenging them to decide anyway, even if the decision is to wait instead of moving on for the time being.

Remember, even if you are wrong about what you sense is blocking their movement or perception, your reflections and questions will help them think for themselves at a deeper level. Share what you think you are receiving from your head, heart, and gut. Then accept and appreciate their responses.

Scientifically, these divisions are simplified because impulses in the neural network are constantly interacting. All parts of the nervous system overlap, making it hard to clearly define where you are sensing from. The practice is to open all three centers before any important conversation, and then notice if you are overusing one center while closing off the others, such as when you are rationalizing your decision, shutting down out of fear, or forcing your ideas on others. Notice, and then quickly reopen your entire nervous system.

You can find a guided visualization to open and align your head, heart, and gut at covisioning.com/coachthepersonresources/.

One final tip for staying in full-body presence: sit up straight. Not only does hunching over and leaning in toward someone crunch your gut, but there is evidence that people who are in a hunched posture for long periods are less assertive. Maarten Bos and Amy Cuddy found that hunching over a smartphone screen or slouching over a laptop actually affects body chemistry and the willingness to be assertive.[4] Their research indicated a hunched-over posture could affect the courage available in subsequent conversations.

Open your mind with curiosity, your heart with gratitude and love, and your gut with courage. Receive what the person is struggling to articulate. They will make many discoveries in this safe container of coaching.

Using Nonreactive Empathy

Empathy doesn't mean getting caught up in people's emotions and dramas. There is a difference between empathy and sympathy. Sympathy is absorbing another's emotions. When sympathizing, you often try to do or say something to ease both your and their discomfort.

Empathy is understanding. *Merriam-Webster* says, "With empathy, you can imagine or understand how someone might feel, without necessarily having those feelings yourself."[5] You have empathy when you witness what they are sharing without judging or analyzing how they are reacting. You accept their distress as a part of the process of seeing themselves and the situation in a different way. You appreciate why they feel the way they do. When people feel safe enough to express themselves because you wholeheartedly recognize and value their experience, they will move into exploration and action more quickly.

You elevate psychological safety by receiving their words and emotions with caring curiosity. You might physically feel their pain or anxiety. Notice these sensations, and then exhale to release the tension so your head, heart, and gut remain open.

You might feel the need to take care of them. It is not your job to fix or heal them. Your job is to help them better understand why they feel what they do and how this relates to what they want to create for themselves going forward. If you interrupt the process by taking care of them with comforting words or advice, or you run to get a tissue without offering it first, you weaken their power. You inhibit their growth. You can break the bond of trust.

Offer what you think they are feeling to see how it matches their experience. They may confirm and offer a different description of what they feel is occurring. Once they are talking about their reaction, ask if they want to stay with it or shift how they feel. If they want to shift, ask what is in their control to change at that moment or in the future that will empower the emotional shift they desire. If they can envision who they will be when they feel differently, you can coach them on what they need to resolve to move into their desired state.

Nonreactive empathy is when you identify, seek to understand, and appreciate what coaches feel, and then let go of feeling their reactions with them.

Most people long to feel seen, heard, and valued no matter what they express. They want to be themselves without judgment. They don't need you to feel sad, stressed, angry, or anxious with them. You can compassionately share what you are sensing and invite them to explore their experience so you both have a better understanding of how their emotions are impacting their thoughts. But if you take in their emotions, your words and expressions will reflect and even amplify the intensity of their reactions. They might feel guilty or sorry for upsetting you. They even might feel they have to take care of you.

> Your job isn't making people *feel* better. You coach them to see better.

Nonreactive empathy helps you feel patient and compassionate. You focus the conversation on them, not you. You remain their thinking partner when you practice nonreactive empathy.

BREAKTHROUGH COACHING RESOURCE
Practicing Nonreactive Empathy

You can practice and develop your nonreactive empathy in any conversation at work or home or out in the world. Remind yourself to practice before you engage. Open your head, heart, and gut, then follow these steps:

1. *Notice when emotions arise in your body*—When you feel a point of tension in your body, try to discern if the emotion is your reaction from what you are sensing your client may be feeling. Use the resource tool in chapter 4, "Tracking Your Daily Emotional States," to help you develop your emotional self-awareness. If you aren't sure if you are sensing their reaction, offer what you are sensing for your client to accept or change.

2. *When asking your client if what you are sensing is correct, tie it to the behavior you noticed*—For example, you could start by saying, "When you paused and looked away, I sensed sadness or confusion. Would you share what you were experiencing?" or "Every time you talk about your current work team, you get agitated. Is there something about your relationship with them you would be willing to explore?"

3. *Quickly own and release your impulse to save the person, fix their problem, or share your own story that you think mirrors theirs*—If you feel bad for them (sympathy) or want to tell them they are right to feel the way they do (commiserate), stay silent. Breathe and return to feeling curious and believing in their ability to move forward with your coaching.

4. *If they have trouble articulating what they are experiencing, test your instinct*—With no attachment to being right, share what you noticed and sensed. For example, you might offer, "It feels as if you are frustrated by not being recognized" or "Your pattern of saying *but* in every sentence has me wondering if your fear of other people's judgments is holding you back." Be quiet until they respond, maintaining a safe space for them to think about your statement.

5. *If they seem confused by what you are offering as a reflection or question, adjust your tactic*—Rephrase your statements more concisely without explaining yourself, or accept they have a different meaning than you thought. Ask them what is important for them in this moment. Let them know you genuinely desire to understand what they are processing.

6. *Shore up your belief in their ability to find a path forward*—Remember, you are there to help them think through their situation so they see what they want to do next. They will feel better if you let them move through their reactions at their own pace. It may take time for them to put the right words to the thoughts and perceptions that are coming up.

CHAPTER 3

Choosing Your Emotions

The emotions you bring into the room and maintain through-out your conversation will facilitate or frustrate the safety your coachees feel. Your emotions impact their willingness to let go of what they think they know so they are open to learn and grow.

Do you know what hijacks your emotional intentions? Can you quickly recognize when you experience a disruptive emotion? Do you know what impulses arise when you are worried your client is judging the value you provide if you don't lead them or give advice?

When reading the testimonials from my first year of coaching, I realized that even though my skills were rough, I provided great value because of the emotions I felt. I gave my clients a safe space to talk through their dilemmas. It might have been the only time in their day they could show up fully as themselves with no fear of judgment.

My acting teacher once told me, "It doesn't matter what the audi-ence thinks of you; you are there to give them 100 percent. For every bit of worry you have about how they are assessing you, you aren't giving them what they paid for."

The first step to practicing emotional choice is to forgive yourself for being imperfect. Only then can you recognize your emotions without being distracted by them.

Emotions show up first in your body before your brain adds thoughts to what is happening. You may quickly hide what you feel, but suppressing emotions still impacts other people's willingness to be fully open and honest with you. The quicker you notice you had a physical reaction, the quicker you can choose to feel compassionately curious instead.

Emotional Saboteurs

Your brain wants you to feel safe. Your patterns of reactions are deeply ingrained. You resist what could feel harmful. You may tend to rush to defensively explain yourself when you feel judged, or you hold your breath and limit your interactions when you feel uncomfortable.

These automatic patterns of behavior are difficult to override. You must develop emotional self-awareness to take back control of your brain. Only then can you see others in a new light, appreciating their perspective and where they are on their learning journey. You also can better recognize and adapt to cultural differences and learning preferences when you catch and release your typical reactions.

I was teaching the pilot leadership program for a global company based in Denmark. The director of human resources was in the back of the room observing the class. The first hour went well. As I began explaining the impact of values on leadership behavior, a few participants challenged the concepts. I offered evidence. Others voiced their opinions and asked for deeper explanations. I felt my neck stiffen as I tried to calmly answer their questions.

At the break, I nearly ran to the back of the room to find out what the director was thinking. Before I could speak, she said, "Wow, they are really engaged!"

I must have looked confused. She added, "Oh, you might not know, this is a great example of how Danes are taught to learn. We challenge teachers we respect, hoping for constructive dialogue." My body relaxed as I realized I was succeeding instead of failing. My assumptions triggered my fears, which could have easily limited my effectiveness as a teacher.

Your emotional saboteurs are related to your social needs. From the time you were born, you repeated behavior that brought you positive attention, love, or safety. You learned how to get what you most needed first from your family. As you began navigating life beyond your family, some behaviors became more significant than others as you sought to feel confident or comfortable in social groups. Getting your needs met fueled your personal or professional successes. These repeated behaviors became your personal strengths. They also became your trigger points.

Your brain wants to protect you when it thinks you won't get your needs met in an upcoming situation or you perceive your need is being disregarded in the moment. Think about the last time you felt irritation, anxiety, or disappointment while interacting with others. What did you expect to get from them that was withheld or disregarded? What about when you led a team meeting or coached a new client that didn't go as you had hoped? Did you feel incompetent? Did you feel useless? Were you angry about their disrespect? Consider what your brain thought you were losing so you might be more objective with your reactions in the future. You will learn more about the strengths and snags of social needs in part 4.

Don't be embarrassed or upset with your impulse to defend yourself, convince others, or shut down. No matter how emotionally mature you think you are, your brain will prompt reactions before your higher self has a chance to intervene.

You might not be able to recognize what need wasn't met in the moment. In reflection, be curious about what transpired so you can learn from the experience. Acknowledging what you thought you needed but didn't get can begin to weaken the control the need has over your brain. This will support your practice of self-awareness and emotional choice while you are interacting.

Exercising Emotional Choice

Because of your brain's quick reaction time, the skill is not to stop yourself from reacting. You want to develop your ability to quickly shift your emotions following a reaction. You can become aware of your emotional reactions and then tell your brain what you would like to feel, think, and do differently. Viktor Frankl said in his book *Man's Search for Meaning*, "Between stimulus and response, there is a space. In that space is our power to choose our response. In our response lies our growth and our freedom."

Noticing that you are reacting is the first step. Take clues from your body. Do you hold irritation in your stomach, shoulders, or jaw? When you are anxious, does your heart beat faster? Does the back of your neck heat up? Your self-awareness gives you the freedom to choose how you want to feel. Then you can choose your emotion, breathing it into your body so the shift is complete.

Developing the mental habit of noticing and shifting your emotions takes time. Consistent practice makes you consistently better. Improve your emotional awareness by setting your phone alarm to go off three times a day for two weeks to remind you to ask yourself, "What am I feeling? Why? Is there something else I'd rather feel right now?"

You have an amazing ability to observe your brain at work. You can even laugh at your brain and then choose to feel, think, and act differently so you don't impair psychological safety from the start to the end of your coaching conversation.

BREAKTHROUGH COACHING RESOURCE
Maintaining a Strong Foundation

Your ability to practice emotional choice is impacted by your states of mind and body. Your diet, sleeping patterns, financial worries, access to friends, and the balance of healthy and unhealthy relationships influence the energy you need to regulate your emotional reactions. The social media conflicts and other noise keep you out of balance. The overwhelming tasks you can't seem to get under control leave you feeling irritated and afraid. Some of us numbly walk through our days, finding nothing to smile about.

You may have picked up some self-care tips that you sometimes follow. After hearing Saundra Dalton-Smith, author of *Sacred Rest*, speak at TEDxAtlanta, I learned that I have a "rest deficit" that impacts my happiness, health, and success.

Dalton-Smith identified seven types of rest we need to feel happy, productive, and fulfilled.[1] She discovered these gaps when diagnosing common ailments in her patients. Helping them get the rest they needed often restored their long-term health.

Sleep is not the same as rest. You won't sleep well if you lack one of the seven types of rest: mental, spiritual, emotional, social, sensory, creative, and physical.

The following are critical habits, which are a combination of Dalton-Smith's work and other ideas that you should develop:

- *Mental rest*—When your mind is tired, you make mistakes and experience memory lapses. The more you let your mind focus on past events you would like to redo and assume worst-case scenarios about future events, the quicker you wear out your brain. When you can, walk outside where it's safe and hopefully quiet. Notice your surroundings. Allow yourself to feel the awe of a beautiful sunset, the bloom of a flower, plants soaking up drops of water from rain, or a child's touch. If you can't go outside, be still or meditate in five-minute blocks. In the evening, it's okay to watch some mindless television to let your brain process what occurred during the day. Hopefully, you will laugh a little before you go to sleep.

- *Spiritual rest*—Spirituality in this context is about your sense of connection to something bigger than yourself. If you don't have a life purpose, you can cultivate a sense of purpose and value when you discover what you do that gives you the pleasure of fulfillment. Maybe your heart feels bigger when you perform an act of kindness for someone else or you have acted toward improving your community or the larger world we live in. Music or uplifting videos can reunite your body-mind-spirit connection. Even an inspiring morning quote can prepare you for the day; consider subscribing to a daily quote from Grateful.org. Journal uplifting moments to preserve them to read when you feel disconnected.

- *Emotional rest*—When my clients express feeling overwhelmed, depleted, or lost, I give them a safe moment to talk, rant, or cry. This exercise releases the pressure that leads to relief and even laughter. To experience this gift, find people you trust who won't judge you or bombard you with advice to talk about the tensions you feel. Also, take breaks at work by saying no when your plate is too full. When you notice you are hesitating to reach out to someone for help, ask yourself what you are afraid will happen. Articulating fears can decrease the power they have over your actions. Then every day, find someone whose positive perspective inspires your own brighter view to be with, even briefly. Hang out with people you tend to smile with when you need an emotional lift.

- *Social rest*—You can feel lonely even around a lot of people. We all need to be seen, loved, and enjoyed by others. Hopefully, you get this from people you can relax with who you aren't afraid will judge you. Make new friends with like-minded people, whether to hike together, read and talk about books, champion a cause, share challenges of your profession, or enjoy the same hobbies as you. Hopefully, you can meet live, but remote gatherings can work if everyone has a chance to safely share their thoughts.

- *Sensory rest*—Most of us are overloaded with noise in our environments, interruptions from our computers and phones, artificial light, stressful driving, and other distractions at work and home. Some restaurant critics even include the noise decibels of restaurants in their reviews. You need to take breaks from your electronics to rest your mind and vision. Immerse yourself in music, get whiffs of fresh air, use aromatherapy or cooking to take in good smells, and rub your hands in things you love to touch to awaken your senses.

- *Creative rest*—Many people lose avenues to express their creativity with age. You might find ways to express your creative talents by taking up a new art or enjoyable hobby. If you like, seek performances of music, dance, and comedy to reawaken your appreciation of beauty and whimsy. Take time to notice details even in mundane environments. You can notice so many wonders as you walk around your neighborhood or favorite place to shop.

- *Physical rest*—Your body needs recovery time whether you are an athlete or you sit in a chair all day. Before your body hurts, spend a few minutes stretching, and take deep breaths throughout your day. When you release tension and calm your body, your productivity and outlook will improve.

Check out the book *Sacred Rest*. You will get tools and tips to get the rest you need plus an assessment at the end of the book to better identify your deficits. This book will not only improve your coaching, it could also save your life.

CHAPTER 4

Catching and Releasing Your Judgmental Reactions

One of the most annoying and nearly impossible demands someone can give you is to say, "Quit being judgmental." Regardless of the strength of your biased opinion, the other person is irritated because you aren't agreeing with their biased opinion. Telling people to stop judging triggers defensiveness, making you both judge each other even more.

Humans are judgmental by nature. Every action you take from the moment you wake is based on what your brain judges as best for you. These automatic judgments are fabricated from your experiences of life to date. Your brain then makes unconscious micro-decisions so you can move through your days without consciously deciding every move you make.

Judging is easy; it doesn't require much thinking. You tend to follow your routines because they are comfortable and deliberation-free. That is why you may forget if you took your morning pill or closed the garage door when, of course, you did. You instinctively avoid what is confusing, difficult, and involuntarily challenging as much as possible.

If you didn't have judgment, it would be difficult to get out of bed every morning. It would be paralyzing to have to think through each choice and action. You activate conscious analysis when uncertainty among options is apparent, you have a need for creativity or a new personal connection, or you are conflicted by your temptations.

Judgments show up in your choice of words and reactions to people. Your brain instantly discerns right from wrong, good from bad, and safe from dangerous based on your past—what you have been taught and what you have discovered from what you have read, heard, or seen. This makes you biased and judgmental.

> One of the best ways of being a better coach and human is to declare, "I am a judgy, biased person."

Generally, you make judgments without malicious intent. Because you mean no harm, you instantly rationalize your judgy remarks and give excuses such as "I didn't mean it that way" or "They don't see the bigger picture." Your defensiveness and justification are meant to protect you.

You could also react negatively when you perceive someone discounting your knowledge or treating you as a child, something family members often do to each other. You may punish offenders in return with your words, anger, or silence. You may not forgive them; your resentment can last for years.

When coaching, your urge to fix, advise, or gently lead coachees to the solution you think is best demonstrates your judgment that they are inadequate. You may start by fully accepting what the person is telling you. You ask questions to determine how the person defines who they are in this situation that might be sabotaging their goals. Then your judgy brain creeps in with the desire to nudge the person in a specific direction for their own good. You don't invite them to choose what they want; you choose for them, assuming that is what they need.

To fully coach the smart, resourceful person you are with, you must recognize your judgments, beliefs, and biases, and then forgive yourself for being human so you can see what else could be real and true for them.

How Do You Know What They Want?

Assuming you know what people want and how they see a situation without making sure your pictures match is a common bad habit of coaches. Even if you have known a person all your life, your assumption that you know what they have in mind even before they finish their sentences is a mistake. Neglecting to ask what key words and emotional shifts mean to them when they vaguely share what they see could cause them to either comply with your statements or react with resistance.

The common assumption of knowing—thinking you know what people mean and want without explanation—is automatic and often wrong. Neurobiologist Steven Rose said, "Our minds/brains develop and create order out of the blooming buzzing confusion . . . thinking we see a snapshot of the brain's current state is meaningless unless we know the *entire life history* of that brain's owner." Rose also said there are no blueprints to rely on, so we are always making up what we think is true about what people tell us.[1]

To limit assumptions about where to go with the session, after coachees describe their dilemma, clarify with curiosity what seems to be the most important words they said. Ask them what the words mean to them. Make sure both of you are clear on what they see when they explain what they mean. Once you have a shared understanding of the meaning they attach to their words and emotions, you can more easily explore what they want that differs from what is occurring now.

If what the client declares they want more or less of is vague and unobservable, such as "to have more confidence" or "to feel more motivated when I wake up," the coach needs to ask the client what having confidence or feeling motivated means to them and what will change when they have these feelings. When vague, unobservable terms are clarified, the coach and client will have an agreement on a vision for the future with fewer assumptions.

If you judge that the outcome they want is clear to both them and you without clarification and agreement, they may enjoy talking about their problems, but the actions they agree to take at the end of the session may not resolve the problem they named at the start. This outcome can shift and change as you address what has been getting in the way of making the changes. You may need to modify the desired outcome of the conversation if something more important to create or change emerges. You need to keep the conversation on track to a destination you both see clearly so you have a yardstick to measure against by the end of the conversation to determine if progress is being made. The steps they commit to take will move them toward what they declared they wanted to create or change.

When clarifying the desired outcome, start by assuming nothing. Do not think you know what they think without checking. Coach them to clearly identify what they understand as their challenge, what they desire to know by the end of the conversation, and what has gotten in the way of knowing what they want and how to get it. Use reflection to ensure you share the same meaning of their words and have the same picture of what they want that they don't have now. This will help you both measure the success of the coaching when you get to the action steps at the end of the conversation.

By giving up the *habit of already knowing* what someone means or wants, you will deepen your connection with them. Stay curious and confirm what you think they mean and want. They will feel seen, heard, and valued.

The Courage to Be Curious

Letting go of knowing takes courage. You have to use willpower to consistently allow yourself to become uncertain. Not knowing can leave you feeling vulnerable. You are a naked nonexpert.

Coaches both new and experienced question their value when they remain completely curious. Trusting the process of coaching doesn't come easily. Even with years of practice, there are still moments when you will want them to see what you think is best for them. It takes courage and deliberate practice to be still and open to what is unfolding.

The best way to activate the courage to coach is to remember that you are cultivating a partnership in a creative process. Letting go of being the expert and instead becoming a partner is the key to coaching. Your joy inspired by this cocreative process can override your urge to help.

The novelist Pico Iyer, having traveled with the Dalai Lama, said the one thing that seemed to give people reassurance and confidence was when the Dalai Lama would answer their questions with, "I don't know."[2] He made it okay for everyone to not know.

Iyer also said, "The opposite of knowledge isn't always ignorance. It can be wonder." In *A Neurophenomenology of Awe and Wonder*, the researchers define wonder as two senses merged: "The first sense is closely tied to the feeling of awe; the second to the feeling of curiosity."[3] In other words, you experience wonder when you see something that takes your breath away and then ponder how this phenomenon came into existence. Add in a little humility for recognizing that everyone you coach is awesome and surprising, then your needs and fears decline as you seek, witness, and accept the shared experience of coaching.

Can you use a sense of wonder to activate your courage? When coaching, can you shift from making quick assumptions about what your coachees mean and need to being curious about how the humans you are with define themselves, their situations, and their desires? Courageously let go of knowing so you can bravely journey together beyond the borders of their stories.

BREAKTHROUGH COACHING RESOURCE

Tracking Your Daily Emotional States

To enhance your coaching sessions, you'll need to learn how to increase your emotional awareness and activate emotional choice.

Emotional reactions are the result of your brain deciding what you should avoid and what makes you happy. Your brain determines what is good, bad, safe, and dangerous based on your past experiences. Your skill is to notice your biological reactions as they occur and then deliberately choose how you want to feel. Emotional choice puts you in control of your brain.

The more adept you are at discerning what is shaping your mood and mental status, the greater you can manage your behavior. However, you are not aware of most of the emotions you experience throughout the day. Most of your feelings exist below the surface of your awareness. To learn and practice the skill of emotional regulation—choosing how you want to feel in the moment—you first need to develop your emotional self-awareness.

For the next two weeks, set your phone or computer to notify you four times a day. Each time quickly tune in to your body and ask yourself the following questions: (1) What am I feeling? (2) What do I think is causing me to feel this way? and (3) What do I want to feel now? Use table 4.1 to help identify what you are feeling. After a few days, look for emotional patterns to determine what circumstances elicit repetitive responses as well as what surprised you.

Assess what you are feeling in the moment instead of relying on memory. Be honest with yourself; nothing is right or wrong about your answers.

TABLE 4.1 List of Emotions

Angry	Annoyed	Anxious	Appalled	Belligerent
	Cheated	Concerned	Contemptuous	Cynical
	Defiant	Distrustful	Envious	Exasperated
	Furious	Hateful	Irritated	Offended
	Outraged	Rebellious	Repulsed	Resentful
	Resistant	Superior	Vengeful	Wary
Fearful	Agitated	Dreading	Edgy	Frightened
	Hesitant	Nervous	Obsessed	Overwhelmed
	Stressed	Threatened	Uneasy	Worried
Disheartened	Abandoned	Apathetic	Baffled	Bored
	Brainless	Burned out	Complacent	Confused
	Defective	Dejected	Depressed	Desperate
	Devastated	Disappointed	Disconnected	Disoriented
	Exhausted	Exposed	Frail	Frustrated
	Gloomy	Grieving	Grumpy	Helpless
	Hurt	Impatient	Isolated	Lonely
	Lost	Moody	Queasy	Sad
	Serious	Shy	Somber	Tired
	Trapped	Unloved	Weak	Weary
Shameful	Aloof	Ashamed	Detached	Embarrassed
	Guilty	Humiliated	Mortified	Reflective
	Regretful	Remorseful	Sorrowful	Uncomfortable
Surprised	Amazed	Astonished	Awestruck	Impressed
	Shocked	Startled	Stunned	

Impassioned	Aroused	Bold	Competitive	Confident
	Crazed	Delirious	Determined	Eager
	Enthusiastic	Euphoric	Excited	Gratified
	Optimistic	Passionate	Thrilled	Willful
Happy	Amused	Appreciative	Blissful	Delighted
	Dreamy	Enchanted	Engrossed	Grateful
	Hopeful	Interested	Intrigued	Joyful
	Lucky	Pleased	Silly	Triumphant
Calm	Accepting	Comfortable	Contented	Forgiving
	Loved	Peaceful	Receptive	Relaxed
	Relieved	Reserved	Satisfied	Serene
Caring	Admiring	Adoring	Affectionate	Compassionate
	Friendly	Generous	Loving	Respectful
	Reverent	Secure	Sympathetic	Tender

Other (write
in your own)

_____ _____ _____ _____

_____ _____ _____ _____

Judgment Field Trip

Judgment is not often defined as an emotion; it is perceived as a thought instead of a physical reaction. Accepting judgment as an emotion means you can track it along with all your emotional states. This exercise will help you discover what judgment feels like so you can develop the ability to shift to feeling curious when judgment arises while coaching.

Instructions

Go to a place where you know your judgment gets triggered, such as the grocery store, the airport, the home of a family member, or a work meeting you dislike attending, and take the following steps:

1. *Notice how your body tenses up*—When you are in environments that disturb you or with people you tend to conflict with, the tension might start even before you walk through the door. Notice when you feel a tightness in your stomach, chest, or neck.

2. *Shift your emotions*—What emotion would allow you to be a neutral witness? Can you feel

patience, curiosity, or even humor? If you need to interact with people, what emotions would help you have a positive experience? Can you feel gratitude, courage, love, or compassion? Breathe in the emotion you want so it fills up your heart.

3. *Catch a judgment relapse*—When you start to feel impatient, anxious, or annoyed, release the tension and return to the emotion you chose to feel instead.

The next time you practice coaching and you are in the role of client, choose to be coached on your experience of catching your judgmental reactions and your attempts to feel something else. Allow yourself to be coached on your stories and long-held beliefs. Explore when you judge yourself for your reactions. Commit to what you will do next in an upcoming challenging conversation or situation.

Developing a practice of catching and releasing judgment will elevate your coaching impact.

PART TWO

Maintaining a Client-Centered Focus

What distinguishes coaching from other problem-solving conversations is you coach what people are thinking about in the moment. You don't start by asking, "What could you try?" or "What are all the possible actions you can take?" They probably can do this analysis on their own. Your coaching can bring options to light throughout the coaching conversation instead of driving the discussion to a quick conclusion. Your focus will be to explore what they want to create that is not currently happening and then what beliefs need to be addressed and what perceived problems need to be resolved so they choose how they want to confidently move toward their desires.

The focus of your coaching is on what defines the person's present perspective. You want to know how they are demarcating the challenge they say they want to discuss and how they see themselves in relation to their dilemma. You want to discover what is getting in the way of this smart person's ability to see or act on options and possibilities. You coach the person's perspective to expand their stories so more answers and actions come into view.

When they begin to clarify the parameters of their story, recap the opinions and assumptions they share, and ask what they think about these beliefs. Restate what they say will negatively happen when they do something or what will happen if they avoid doing something that others expect them to do. Be curious about their use of the words *never* and *always*. Seeing their thinking in your reflections helps them recognize the gaps in their logic and the justifications they unconsciously repeat to avoid taking risks.

You don't try to fix them with advice or lead them to the "correct" answer. You don't need to find patterns from their past or envision a perfect future. You summarize what you think are key statements they shared, using their words, and ask follow-up questions that prompt them to examine the map of their thinking. Then they can see how the paths they are on serve them now and what roadblocks may be slowing them down or blocking their movement. Most likely they will see a new a path forward that feels more meaningful and inspiring.

This is the gift of coaching. The human brain doesn't like uncertainty, so we create a crutch of what we believe to be true based on past experiences so we don't feel as if we are walking on shaky ground. But certainty closes off the mind. Writer Ephrat Livni described the fallacy of knowing and the need for understanding in her article "It's Better to Understand Something Than to Know It." Livni said, "Knowing is static, referring to discrete facts, while understanding is active, describing the ability to analyze and place those facts in context to form a big picture."[1] Coaching expands the context so people understand the situation beyond what they think they know, providing a two- and even three-dimensional portrayal of themselves and their situation. The lightbulb pops on as creative insights come into view. The new awareness leads to growth.

The end result of coaching will provide new ways of seeing and solving problems, but the focus is on the person's thinking, so they see what they can do differently on their own. The discovery process embeds the learning and commitment to act.

The coachee is focused on their problem; you are focused on the story they are telling about the problem. You listen and observe the client to discover cracks in the story you can use to break through the frames so a new story appears.

CHAPTER 5

How to Shift to Coach the Person While Seeking to Solve a Problem

I f you were running down a path and encountered a wall you could not see how to climb or go around, what would you do? Wouldn't it be nice if you could call someone to help you think through how best to contend with the wall so you could continue down the path? That is what a coach does best.

No matter how smart and experienced you are, your brain gets stuck in old thinking patterns that block the view of how to resolve complex, and sometimes even simple, dilemmas. Most people resist objectively evaluating how they see situations and themselves. The smarter you are, the more adept you are at justifying why you do what you do instead of looking for gaps.[1] It's easier to blame others, the economy, or other obligations for your inaction. If you can't explain why the wall in front of you exists, you might rant about the stupid decision the wall builders made. Or worse, you might blame yourself for not being smart enough to avoid the path in the first place.

The brain's desire to quickly explain a situation and establish why the dilemma is difficult to resolve is the reason why coaching starts with listening to the person's story instead of giving advice. Historian and author Rutger Bregman said we stick to narrowly defining experiences because "We are what we believe. We find what we go looking for."[2] Instead of trying to fix a problem when a person is resisting seeing it from another angle, coaches start by listening for their client's definitions and rationalizations holding the pieces of the story together. Simply asking what key words mean to them and the reasoning behind their perceptions begins the restructuring process that could transform their thinking.

Telling people what is wrong with their thinking only raises their defenses. The more emotions attached to a storyline, the harder it is to detach from the hold the story has on their choices. They first need to trust that you see their point of view. Then they might open up to hearing your reflections and answering your questions, leading to new ways of seeing and thinking.

Once they trust you aren't making them wrong with your feedback and you accept their emotional reactions and perceptions as right for them, you can begin to break their stories into pieces that can be objectively observed. They will allow themselves to engage with you as you highlight the beliefs holding their stories in place. They will thoughtfully answer your questions intended to differentiate facts from assumptions. The associations they then make will lead to breakthroughs in their stories, the lightbulb moments needed to see what they can do next to move forward.

A study done in April 2022 in Spain recorded activity in the regions of the brain thought to be associated with problem-solving. Researchers studied three different approaches with each participant: (1) solitary sorting, (2) receiving direct opinions and advice, and (3) nondirective coaching using reflections and open-ended questions. Not only did the study demonstrate that different areas of the brain were activated by each of the approaches, but the coach approach also led to the highest activity in the region of the brain associated with creativity. The participants generated far more insights they called *aha moments* that enhanced their problem-solving capacity than when trying to figure something out on their own or when they were told what was best to do.[3]

The study confirmed when you coach a person's thinking instead of just focusing on alternate ways to solve a problem, the creative insights that emerge accelerate the change process. People not only see new ways to proceed but also do so with more confidence and often more excitement.

How to Use Coaching to Activate Creative Thinking

For clients to know what else could be occurring outside the stories they are holding on to, they need the narrative laid out in front of them like a picture book they can study. As they describe what they see, your summaries of what they share and your questions that stem from your curiosity of their choices supports a generative conversation that leads to new insights. Holding the story outside their heads activates the creative process.

You receive and share back what they express with as little interpretation as possible. You may summarize key elements and offer a word you think encapsulates what they think is holding them back, but you offer these statements and words for their review. You may be wrong. Even declining your offer because it's not correct will help them look more deeply into their thoughts.

The discoveries they make are called *breakthroughs* because the process of reflecting their experience and tactfully questioning their thinking breaks down the fears, doubts, and resentment holding the story in place. This process stimulates their brain activity instead of pacifying it with advice. You broaden their capacity to think and then act more confidently at that moment and in the future.

You start with feeling compassionately curious. Never assume you know what others mean when they tell you what they see and feel. They must verbalize the meaning of their words and how they fit into their perspective so you can observe what they see and think. When you seek this understanding, they begin observing their thinking as well. You do this with an open mind and compassionate heart so they aren't afraid of your judgment. They know you are there for their higher good. Your intentions are for their growth, not your success.

> Compassion is the energy they feel from you when you respect, care for, and enjoy the amazing human you have the honor of coaching.

Compassion can also activate your courage when coaching. You are more willing to share when people say what they want and then later say something contradictory to their original statements. You can also lift them out of the story they keep going back to by asking them to clearly state what they need at that moment. You care enough to challenge them to name the possibilities suppressed by their protests or hidden beneath the rock of their regrets.

You don't have to be an experienced coach to make a difference for them. Even if you are new to coaching, facilitating their thinking with some reflections and questions in a safe space where they can think out loud is extremely helpful. They can observe and analyze their thinking in a way they can't do for themselves if you use compassionate curiosity to share what you notice and ask clarifying questions that encourage mental examination.

In other words, don't try too hard to be a good coach. Don't think about what you are going to say before you say it. If people don't understand your question or hesitate as they try to fit your statement into their perspective, just ask if you can rephrase what you said. It often comes out better the second time around, especially if you remember to use their phrases in your reflection and their words in your questions.

Simple reflections help them see their thinking outside their head. Reflecting and confirming what you hear as their doubts and beliefs helps them evaluate the source of their decisions and actions. As they begin to detach from the story they held so tightly, they accept what has hindered their thinking and see what they need to do next.

Once they see what steps they can take to move forward, they feel a commitment to act. If you then ask them when they will implement the step they declared and what they will do if the result isn't quite what they hope for, the declaration becomes a promise to themselves. They know what to do and how to forgive themselves for mistakes as a part of their growth.

Seek to Transform, Not Fix

Don't make your coachee do anything at the start of the session other than talk. You open the door with a generic question, such as "What is on your mind today?" or "What challenge would you like to explore?" Simply asking them what is on their mind to start the conversation puts the coaching into motion.

Then listen to their story knowing you aren't there only to resolve a problem but also to transform *how they are thinking*, which might reveal better options than what they had considered. They need to say what they haven't spoken out loud. They need to recognize aspects of the situation they hadn't taken into account. They need to expand the boundaries of their story to diffuse the limiting beliefs, fading hopes, and outside opinions influencing their decisions.

Be careful of the trap of only talking about what went wrong and what they should do next. These conversations can be useful, but they are transactional discussions that change only what the person will do differently. It's likely they can figure this out on their own if they take the time to list their options, risks, and gains on paper.

Your first intent is to ensure you have shared understandings of what they see as difficult, what label they are giving to their feelings, and what they declare they want to have or feel instead of what is occurring at that moment. You do this by summarizing key points and words and asking what these words mean to them. To *see into* their thinking, you must give up what you think you already know so you can clearly understand what they are talking about.

I was coaching a woman who said she wanted to know how to support her adult daughter making a difficult life transition. I was going to ask her what she meant by support when she said with what felt like a sense of urgency mixed with despair, "I want to know what is right for me to do as her mother." I shared that I felt the importance of her deep desire and then asked her who held the definition of *good mother*. After a long pause, she said, "I guess my daughter does." I then asked her what supporting her daughter at that moment might look like. She sighed and said, "I don't need to know. I need to ask her." What may seem obvious from the outside is often fogged with fear and yearning inside the mind.

Offering your observations and asking about key words is an invitation for your coachees to evaluate, confirm, or modify their thinking. You might use phrases that start with "It sounds like what you want to change is . . ." or "You mentioned your biggest fear was . . ." or "You said the main thing you aren't getting right now is . . ." or "You hesitated for a moment and then changed what you said you wanted to focus on . . . Would you share what changed your mind?" Then you wait for and accept their response.

Your follow-up question may be to determine meaning, significance, or direction of the conversation. You might ask something such as "Is this what is most important to you?" or "These words seemed to stand out for you. Is there anything I missed?" or "I can tell you are irritated and want the result to be different. You keep looking at how you can change things, even though they said the decision was final. Would it be helpful to look deeper into your disappointment, or do you want to look at what you could do next?"

Your use of reflective inquiry at the beginning of the conversation brings the story forward. Helping them see their thinking even in the first few minutes of the coaching session will lead to expanding the scope of their story. The lightbulb often comes on when they say, "Wow, that's crazy! I need to stop this." Then you can start looking at what needs to be addressed to create a new story that supports their strengths and desires.

 **BREAKTHROUGH COACHING RESOURCE**

Bringing the Nuts and Bolts of the Story into View

Although the bulk of your coaching is a spontaneous exploration that emerges as you clear clients' mental clutter, the coaching session starts and ends with a deliberate action by you as the coach. You want to agree on where the conversation is going and what will happen next.

Open the coaching session by asking the client to talk about what is on their mind. Share the desires and beliefs you hear them use to frame their story, seeking to discover what is most important for them to create and what they think is stopping them from having what they want. The bulk of the coaching is discovering what needs to be resolved so they can achieve their desired outcome, leading to the next steps they will take to positively move in that direction.

I usually don't recommend using a list or trying to remember questions when coaching. However, reviewing these two lists before you go into a coaching session might help remind you how to effectively coach the way they think instead of starting the session by focusing on actions to take.

Note: Remember to put these lists of questions away before you coach so you stay fully present while coaching.

Beliefs Formed from Past Experiences

Beliefs Formed from Past Experiences

Reflect on what stands out as most important in their story, and ask questions to make sure you understand what they mean by their words and reactions:

- "What do you mean when you said . . . ?"
- "What do you believe is driving the behavior (of the boss, colleagues, friends, family) that seems to be holding you back?"
- "You said you felt . . . What happened that made you feel this way?"
- "If you were to make a decision or determine a plan, what do you hope to have as a result of the decision or plan that feels important to you now?"
- "How are other people's opinions or external circumstances affecting your ability to achieve what you most desire?"
- "How would you like for people to see you if you fully stepped into the person you want to be?"

Assumptions about What Will Happen and Why

Assumptions about What Will Happen and Why

Reflect on what you hear they expect will happen or fear will never happen, and ask questions to explore what they are basing their ideas on:

- "What is happening now that indicates what will happen in the future?"
- "How have you tested your assumptions to determine how valid they are?"
- "What else is possible for you that you hesitate saying out loud?"
- "What do you need to let go of to see more possibilities in the future?"
- "What do you know for sure will never happen?"
- "When facing the uncertainty and obstacles that exist today, what will you most regret not doing a year from now?"

CHAPTER 6

What Are You Listening for That Can Lead to a Breakthrough?

I was mentoring a coach using a recording plus a written transcript of the session for review. We watched the recording together so I could be specific with my observations.

When the coach asked the client what she wanted to talk about, the client began by saying she was not happy with how her life had turned out. She has a job, but she doesn't feel good about it at the end of the day.

The coach said, "So you have a job you don't like."

I paused the recording to tell the coach that the client offered two topics, but instead of inviting the client to choose the challenge she wanted to explore, the coach chose for her. The client had said she didn't like how her life had turned out, and she said she didn't like her job. The coach chose to focus on the job. My suggestion was to share with the client the two things she said she didn't like to see if they were separate issues or interrelated. I offered this possible invitation as an example: "You said you aren't happy with how your life turned out. You also said you don't like the job you are doing now. Are these two different challenges to look at separately—the direction of your life and finding a job that makes you feel good at the end of the day?" The answer would begin to set the framework for the coaching. Trust that the client will determine if the topics are two separate ones or are connected and need to be explored together.

We resumed watching the recording. When the coach asked the client what she didn't like about her job that she would like to change, the client said, "I just don't want to be in my job every day, in that work environment. I am not able to do my best work. I'd like to give my all, to want to give my best to my job. But why don't I feel like giving my all to this job? The people are okay. My boss is supportive. But I barely notice anyone or anything as I rush through the halls. I am not sure—is it that I have too many things to do or that I want to be a part of something bigger, something that gives me a sense of purpose? Can I find this feeling in a nine-to-five job? I do like the part of project management where I'm helping teams and people achieve what they want. I guess I'm just not sure what I want and if I can find it with the company I work for now."

The coach then said, "Tell me more about what you don't like about your work environment."

When I asked the coach why he chose to focus on her environment, he said, "I was trying to reflect her words she used to explain what her challenge is and be curious about the meaning of what she shared." In other words, the coach was trying to do something technically correct but missed the essence of the lack of fulfillment the client was feeling that was making her work a challenge.

Together, we looked at the written transcript of the recorded coaching session. I asked him to pull out the questions the client asked in the paragraph. He said that she asked, "But why don't I feel like giving my all to this job?" and "I am not sure—is it that I have too many things to do or that I want to be part of something bigger, something that gives me a sense of purpose? Can I find this feeling in a nine-to-five job?"

I asked the coach if these were the questions she was seeking answers to and what was the challenge she was beginning to define that he could further explore with her. The coach said if he could do it over, he would ask her to explain what she thinks might help her "feel like giving my all to a job" or ask her if she would like to explore what "being a part of something bigger" might look like in a job she could do at that moment. The coach then said the conversation would probably have been more about the direction her life was taking and what values and purpose were not being honored. The client could then determine what job would motivate her to give her all.

The coach said what he learned from the mentoring was to listen for the patterns in the conversation, especially when coachees ask themselves questions. In this case, the pattern indicated her desire to discover what would motivate her in a job at this moment in her life. He needed to zoom out to see the entire story in the context of her life and sense of value and purpose, not zoom in on the details that just further described the specifics of the story.

The Seeds That Reveal the Direction of the Session

It is better to relax into your curiosity as you take in your clients' story instead of grabbing a word or concept to demonstrate that you are listening. What seems to be most important that is causing concern? What are they most confused about that has triggered their doubt or worry? What questions are they asking themselves? Dig deeper for what they mean when they start naming what they want to know.

It doesn't matter if you ask the perfect question. You won't coach well if you feel you need to meet an expectation or gain their admiration. Self-judgment contaminates your coaching presence. Author Anne Lamott said, "You get your intuition back when you make space for it, when you stop the chattering . . . mind." When you must think about what to say, you "squeeze out much that is rich and juicy and fascinating."[1]

Although you should not worry how your words will land, you should beware when your coachees use the time just to talk and then thank you for what they discovered on their own. They did value having a safe space to verbally process their ideas, but did you help them explore beyond their cognitive restructuring of easily accessible thoughts? You still want to ask them if they would be willing to examine what they mean and see before following a path that feels good. You might feel you are interrupting the flow or bringing down the energy, but if you remember your purpose for coaching, you need to ask if they would look deeper to make sure they see the whole story before committing to a plan.

When commenting on creativity in a 1997 interview, David Bowie said you should never feel safe or complacent: "Always go a little further into the water than you feel you're capable of being in. Go a little bit out of your depth, and when you don't feel that your feet are quite touching the bottom, you're just about in the right place to do something exciting."[2] I believe his wise words apply to the creative process of coaching.

Even when people just keep talking, you can interrupt if you ask permission and tell them you are hoping to better understand something they just said. Then be willing to name the contradiction you heard when they had said one thing about their desires followed by something opposite. Challenge their judgments of themselves when they say they want to do something and then follow it up with a phrase starting with the word *but*. Is the *but* a reality to address or a fear keeping them stuck? Directly state when they have gotten off track, asking if they want to maintain focus on the outcome they agreed to earlier or if something else has emerged that feels more important.

You will begin to hear what needs are haunting them or what they are longing for but don't feel they are worthy of receiving or believe is within their reach. You will notice the sputtering of excuses when they are afraid to use their courage to let go of obligations pinning them in a place they don't want to be.

Listen to their diatribe as they circulate old thoughts, trying to spin something new out of what they already know. You will hear what is just below the surface that wants to come out but is still a blind spot for them. Offer what you think is there. Be silent as they think about what you offer and what it might mean to them right now. This is how you cocreate their awareness and reality.

How Are You Listening?

Good listening takes effort. If you tend to think about what people are saying and consider what you may say next, you need to be aware of how you are listening. Then when you start thinking too much, you can breathe and relax into your body so you don't miss something important.

Listening expert Julian Treasure differentiated *critical listening* from *empathic listening*.[3] He said when we listen critically, we listen to evaluate what we hear, gauge the value of the information, and form our own opinion of what was said. We might do this kind of listening to gather facts to solve a problem. You may even get impatient listening to details that you feel won't help fix the problem.

Empathic listening, Treasure noted, is intended to support the speaker's feelings and help them feel safe, valued, and respected. When you feel compassion—when you respect, care for, and enjoy the person you have the honor to coach—you activate empathic listening to fully understand how they are experiencing their situation. They open up and share freely, knowing you won't judge them. You open up to learning what they see and why.

Empathic listening isn't chatting for the sake of connection. You are still looking to drill down to what people want to create or change. We will look at how to crystallize what clients truly want as the desired outcome of the coaching session in part 3.

Coaching is a spontaneous interaction that often leads to greater self-awareness more than goal achievement, but you keep the end in mind to make sure they are addressing what is hindering their evolution.

Follow these tips when using empathic listening in a coaching conversation:

- *Start by genuinely seeking to understand the person's perspective*—It's not enough to just nod your head, smile, and make eye contact if the session is live or make confirming noises if you are talking by phone. They must feel you are interested in their perspective, not trying to manipulate their judgment.
- *Summarize and ask about what you hear so they feel you are listening*—With care and genuine curiosity, restate what you think are the key points they shared and ask open-ended questions about the meaning and importance of the points, such as "What do you mean by wanting to feel more motivated?" or "Say more about why you won't say the right things in the meeting" or "What makes finding a way to have a different relationship important to you now?"
- *Accept their emotions as normal human reactions*—Release your tension and judgment when people get emotional. As they process their experience, feelings may emerge. Remain calm and silently hold a safe, caring space until the emotional reaction subsides. Don't try to save them or push them too soon. Breathing while you pause and remembering that you care encourages them to share with you what they experienced when they feel ready to talk.
- *Ask how their anger, frustration, or lingering hurt is getting in the way of moving on*—For example, you can ask, "What

need was not met or ignored in your last job (or relation-ship)?" "Is there a regret that needs self-forgiveness?" "You suddenly got quiet—is there something you are thinking about but not saying?" Let their answers surface. They may need some time and your silence before they are able to articulate the sources and impact of their emotions on what they now see.

- *Ask how might the person's self-concept be in conflict with their desires*—How are they defining their role and contribution? Do they need to reevaluate who they can be now to succeed? Often, people get stuck in separating who they were in the past from who they can be today.

- *If the person is stuck while making a major life choice, ask what brings them the most joy or sense of fulfillment at work or in their personal life*—Ask them to describe moments in the past when they felt most alive and happy. Can they find ways to bring these moments into their days or into a vision of what their life could be a year from now? Can these moments help them define a meaningful mission or sense of purpose? What do they most value that they have left behind? Can they find a way to align their highest values going forward? Knowing how they can lean into their heart to hear their deepest desires can be more uplifting than disappointing. The reali-zation of an inspiring vision can quiet the fears that come up when considering the risks.

How to Tell If You Are Reflecting or Interpreting Their Meaning

Often when I'm mentoring a coach, I ask them if they noticed when the coachee expressed an emotional shift. The answer is often "Yes, but I wasn't sure how to say what I noticed without sounding judg-mental. What if it is just my personal interpretation?" They hope I will give them a quick, easy answer for knowing if their thinking is getting in the way, but I can't.

Even if you have developed your capacity for empathy, you may still have difficulty discerning the difference between clean reflection and intellectual invention. The actual source of your words might not matter because you are offering only what you observed with curiosity, not certainty. They can then confirm, deny, or alter what you offer with their words or reactions. Then you can explore what they think about what you said.

Over time, you can develop your reflective capacity like the muscles in your body; you bring your senses alive with consistent exercise. Throughout the day, practice full-body presence. Plant your feet on the ground, and shift your awareness into your body. Go outside, open your arms wide, and look up at the sky. Feel the fullness of your heart and the warmth generating from your center as you sense you are a part of this amazing universe.

Practice making this shift in awareness a few times a day. You will naturally take your practice into your conversations. Not only will you be able to better hear your coachees' needs, fears, and what they long for, they will also trust you are wholeheartedly there for them.

BREAKTHROUGH COACHING RESOURCE

Three Tips for Clarifying the Challenge and the Desire

Follow these three tips when clarifying the challenge and the desire:

Reflect so they say *That is right* or *No, I mean this.*	Ask about indications of their desires, fears, and conflicts of values.	Be curious about who they want to be in the future.
Use brief summary statements using their words and expressions so they examine their thoughts, not your interpretation of their meaning. Start with "So you are saying . . ." or "It sounds as if . . ." or "You said this a few times. Would you tell me more about what you mean or want?" They need to objectively observe their stories to assess what's inside.	While telling their stories, listen for the words *really, but,* and *should.* Reflect the phrases that follow these words, then ask questions such as "Is this what you want to create?" (after *really*). "Is this the doubt holding you back?" (after *but*) or "Is this about your fear of being judged for your choices?" (after *should*).	When they share what they want to create, ask them who they need to be to make their desire a reality. If they envision a day doing what gives them joy and fulfillment, what are they feeling when speaking to others and doing their best work? What strengths are they using? What impact do they have on others? Can they begin being this person now?

CHAPTER 7

The Value of Reflecting Emotional Expressions

We often count on people to tell the truth when sharing what they know about themselves. *Truth* is not the word to use, however; you can hope they will be candid with what they see, but they likely can't give you a total, impartial description. You're better off asking people if they would take a moment to consider and then share how they define themselves in a specific role or situation that day. You might ask them to list their strengths, their mismatches, what they value about themselves, and what they do well or would like to do better, especially under stress.

Self-reports are based on perception and impacted by both self-criticism and aspiration. They may tell you the truth about what they see in the moment, but their assessment is both skewed and incomplete. Even if you have permission to survey or interview other people to gather perceptions of your coachee, the results are subjective opinions and biased evaluations based on the questions asked and the history of the relationship.

When asking people to describe who they see themselves being in a situation, they are likely to label their role or dominant pattern of behavior. Their emotions will impact their disclosure. They might have aspects of themselves they resist facing, creating blind spots or safe facades that could even surprise them when revealed. They might be uncomfortable divulging an embarrassing trait or a flaw they worry will cause you to negatively judge them.

> To look into how their story is impacting their choices and behavior, reflecting the emotions that guard self-disclosure is an effective way to draw out their personal truth.

You were born with the ability to recognize when you are experiencing an emotion but not the ability to understand and describe the feeling in words. Small children often bite, hit, kick, throw items, cry, or scream when experiencing strong emotions. As you grow up, you might learn how to talk about and cope with emotions in a more socially appropriate manner. However, you likely weren't given adequate tools, training, or compassionate enough to fully develop your emotional recognition. In most cultures, children and adults are either chastised or quickly soothed when displaying what is seen as negative emotions. For survival, you learned to hide your emotions or blame others for feeling the way you do to justify your expression.

Believing in the evils of certain emotions leads people to ignore what they are feeling. It is normal for people to more easily talk about what they are thinking than feeling, but emotions impact perception and choices, so when you witness a demonstration of an emotion or an apparent shift in expression, you want to ask coachees if they would be willing to share what they are feeling in the moment and explore what the expression means to see how they view the challenges they are describing. This query will help them understand what is motivating their thoughts and actions.

Attempting to bring their emotional experience into the conversation is an important part of being their thinking partner. Their protective brain has inhibited talking about their feelings, or it distorts their reasoning when trying to sort through their experience on their own. Your coaching can help them see through their fog of fear, remorse, and disappointment to discover the impact their emotions have on their relationships, job performance, and overall happiness.

The Power of Noticing Emotional Shifts

The people you coach are constantly telling you how they feel through their nonverbal cues. Their facial expressions, shifts in posture, where they put their hands, volume changes in their voice, and when they look away or glare at you are clues that something else is going on in their minds that needs to be put into words. Reflecting these cues can prompt them to speak about what they are experiencing.

Instead of asking, "What are you feeling?" share what you notice and ask if they would be willing to look at what the expression means to them right now. They may more readily divulge what was difficult to look at when they first told you their story about the challenge they want to explore.

When coaching people through problems or indecision, sharing what you noticed as an emotional shift can be more enlightening than the follow-up question. When I summarize what people tell me and ask if this best describes what is going on, they stop and *think about their thinking.* When I notice and share a shift in their body and energy, they stop and *think about their feelings.* Then, when they seek to understand the reason for their reaction, they may substantiate or alter the beliefs or fears that were blocking their view.

You may also notice the contradictions between their words and body language, such as when they say they are sure about something, but their voice reflects hesitation. They speak more softly or slowly. Maybe they say they are okay with someone's behavior, but their muscles tighten up. Asking about these discrepancies can encourage revelation.

Reflecting techniques go beyond hearing their words. When you are fully present and not thinking about what they are saying, you can receive what they offer with their gestures and energy. Reflecting these shifts creates lightbulb insights and initiates transformation.

How to Share the Shifts You Notice

Sharing the nonverbal expressions or shifts in energy you notice can be jarring. It can also be the best way to get coachees to think about what they are thinking, what they are believing and assuming, and the reality of their expectations and then admit to what they really want to do that they felt uncomfortable telling anyone before.

When they look away, suddenly become quiet, or get frustrated with the conversation, offer your observation graciously, and invite them to share what they think prompted the shift. Say something like, "You suddenly looked away as if something sprang into your mind. Would you share that thought with me?" or "You got louder and talked faster, as if there is a sense of urgency. Is something else coming to mind?" or after a long period of silence, ask, "Would you be willing to talk about what is coming up for you now?" Concisely offering what you observe with a follow-up invitation to look into the reaction deepens the conversation.

As always, be prepared for your assessment to be wrong. If you are wrong, they will correct you, which leads them to think more deeply about their thoughts and feelings.

As the conversation incorporates their emotional reactions, be sure to check in to see if the outcome the person wanted to create still holds. Repeat the desired outcome they stated, and ask if anything has changed. Is the outcome still relevant? Is there something else that feels more important to focus on? Bringing suppressed emotions to the surface can open up a larger conversation around fulfillment, happiness, and life purpose. Clients more comfortably state what does and doesn't truly matter in this situation anymore.

Walking with Clients through Darkness to Light

Exploring emotional shifts won't always be comfortable, but the clarity from understanding the source of emotional reactions leads to making confident choices. You aren't there to be a cheerleader or make sure they always feel confident and positive. Remember, you don't coach to make them feel better. You coach to help them see better.

Insights often emerge from the discomfort that accompanies an opening in their awareness. For a moment, they feel awkward and uncertain. They may feel embarrassed when they realize the impact of their behavior on others or themselves. They may feel sad they haven't realized this before. They may get angry or defensive. The intensity of the emotion will subside if you stay compassionately silent until they begin to breathe normally again.

Your silence provides a safe space for them to express themselves freely. They are learning about themselves in this mind-opening moment. The most difficult times in our lives come from transitioning from one version of ourselves to another. The process of unknowing to knowing can feel scary. Clients need you to sit still with them as they experience the breakthrough, recouping and claiming what they suddenly see.

If you notice your own discomfort with their emotions, breathe and relax so you can stay present and open. You will miss the opportunity to explore the meaning of the expression if you shut down. You might even break their trust in you if you try to move on or make them feel better so you can feel better too.

If your body tightens up with judgment or fear due to your own biases, take another breath and slowly exhale while you clear your mind. Remind your heart to warmly regard the person in front of you who is trusting you to help them solve a dilemma.

Use nonreactive empathy to compassionately detach from their emotions. Experience their reaction, but then let the feeling float away so you don't get lost in their story and experience. You can say that you understand why they feel this way without trying to heal them. You remain the witness so you can stay present and coach them when they are ready to talk about what they are experiencing and seeing now.

BREAKTHROUGH COACHING RESOURCE

Tip Sheet for Recognizing Emotional Shifts

Emotions are not bad or sad, they are energy moving through the body. Your observations and questions need to be judgment-free.

Typical shifts can include any of the following:

- Looking down or away as people change their tone of voice
- Hesitating or becoming silent
- Getting louder or more animated
- Stressing the words *always* or *never* when describing other people's intentions or behavior
- Using the word *really* accompanied by a heightened tone that accentuates a declaration, such as "What I *really* want" or "What I *really* can't stand"

You can challenge people's thinking after an emotional reaction, but don't push, coax, or try to fix their situation based on what they share.

Here are some examples of pushing versus challenging statements a coach might make:

- *Pushing*: "The other person needs to know the impact their behavior and expectations is having on you. Do you have the courage to tell them?"
- *Challenging*: "You paused and looked away as you started to tell me how hurt and emotionally abused you feel in this

situation. Without blaming yourself for what is occurring, what door is opening for you now?

- *Pushing:* "You said you needed to make a change but now stiffened up with resistance as you said you can't. Why are you letting your guilt hold you back?"

- *Challenging:* "You said earlier you needed to make a change so you can do your best work in a more supportive environment. Just now your body stiffened up and your voice sounded a bit defensive as you listed why you can't make the change now. Do you want to look at how important it is for you to honor the *shoulds* you just mentioned?"

- *Pushing:* "You know that if you just accept what you have is a bad idea, then you will stay stuck forever. Why don't you just go for what you want?"

- *Challenging:* "I hear your struggle with making this choice. A year from now, which decision will you most regret not making?"

- *Pushing:* "I know you can do this. You aren't too old. Get over yourself and jump!"

- *Challenging:* "You said you have acted courageously when looking at your options in the past. What is stopping you now?"

CHAPTER 8

How to Coach Insights out of Emotional Moments

After an online coaching demonstration, one of the observers asked the client, "The coach made the same observation three times: 'You seem to already know what to do about the problem you named. What are you really worried will happen when you return to work from your sick leave?' How did that make you feel when the coach asked the same question three times?"

The client answered, "Annoyed. Not with the repetition but my sense she could see right through me. I know what to do. I'm just afraid I'll fail. I could make myself sick again if I were to let my brain keep spinning. She quieted the noise enough for me to muster the courage to try."

After a pause, the client added, "I never thought she was impatient with me. I didn't like being held to the fire, but no matter how much I squirmed, she stayed solid. Her courage fired up mine."

This interaction demonstrates how coaching people to expand their awareness is often uncomfortable but important. The reaction to bringing outdated beliefs to light registers somewhere between slight discomfort and an emotional outpour. The truth can hurt, or at least be an unexpected surprise, before it sets them free.[1]

> Unpleasant feelings are just as crucial as the enjoyable ones in helping make sense of the choices we make.

Someone expressing emotions in coaching is a good sign. Emotions can open the door to learning. Emotions trigger a restructuring of thoughts, creating the lightbulb moment. A clearer and broader understanding of the situation can emerge. Giving coachees a safe, judgment-free space to observe how they are experiencing life in this moment is critical to their progress.

Emotions and the Creative Brain

Many researchers still support the four stages of creativity identified by Graham Wallas in 1926: preparation, incubation, illumination, and verification.[2] Although people can discover answers through a problem-solving approach of exploring options and risks, when they have an aha moment where an insight illuminates a new awareness, what they discover exists outside the boundaries of their stories. They go beyond recirculating thoughts they already know to creating new ideas. Coaching is a creative process.

The creative spark in coaching occurs when the frames protecting an old story are cracked open and an insight bursts through. The frames are held together by emotions such as fear, doubt, guilt, embarrassment, and resentment. The stronger the emotions, the more rigid the frames. These emotions calcify the frames of their stories. It takes an external disruptor—the coach—to break down the frames allowing the creative process to occur.

You use your presence to establish safety and trust necessary to facilitate this process. Your courageous presence also encourages them to step outside their comfort zones as realizations often evoke powerful emotional reactions.

Let's look closer at the four stages of creativity I adapted for coaching using Wallas's work: exploration, focusing in, illumination, and confirmation.

Stage 1: Exploration

When you reflect the words clients use, they are prompted to think about their thinking, which is an analytical process of examining the meaning of their words in the context they are exploring, how their thoughts serve or delay reaching their goals, and what other ways of thinking are possible. According to psychologist Shelley Carson, this process stimulates *intellectual curiosity*.[3] You start coaching here, examining the information clients provide at an intellectual level. You listen to their story, seek to understand their perspective, and begin to clarify what they want instead of what is occurring at that moment.

Gathering information is the first stage of the creative process. Then the conversation takes a deeper dive as you explore what needs to be resolved or addressed to progress toward the desired outcome.

Stage 2: Focusing In

Once the desired outcome is clarified, coaching shifts to exploring what needs to be addressed or resolved to achieve the outcome. When looking at what is blocking forward movement, the conversation moves from an intellectual discourse to eliciting emotionally charged reasoning and rationalizations. The focus of your curiosity shifts from external definitions to internal emotional states and triggers.

When looking at challenges, you wonder, "What is stopping this capable person from solving this problem on their own?" The clues come from their bodily reactions.

There are cultural differences in the expression of emotions, but all humans experience emotional reactions. As you coach people to consider the source of their challenges, they may feel fear, anger, or embarrassment as they face what they have been avoiding. As you coach them to declare what they actually want and don't want at this moment, they may be surprised with the intensity of their voice or the quick and certain firmness in their responses. Their reactions may be obvious or subtle. Either way, when you share what you noticed and ask what their reactions mean, a new view of their dilemma emerges.

Noticing and sharing emotional shifts sets off a different reaction when the new awareness emerges. Psychologist Mark Beeman of Northwestern University led a study in 2004 that measured people's brain activity during flashes of insight. The moment a new connection is made, the brain experiences a burst of activity that is less involved in processing the new information as it is reacting to the surprising insight.[4]

The process includes a moment where the client looks lost in thought as the brain quickly makes new connections to incorporate the breakthrough awareness. When the connections are made, the person reacts emotionally, which may include anger, sadness, or even elation.

Don't interrupt the process. Stay silent, and witness the magic.

Stage 3: Illumination

Don't ask, "What are you feeling?" Clients likely can't name their reaction, or they choose a word they can easily justify. Instead, share the shift you noticed or felt, such as when they looked away and paused, looked down as they expressed regret, quickly changed the subject, or made their voice louder when they talked about the latest project their boss dumped on them. After you share what you noticed, ask if they would share what thoughts triggered the shift.

Consider the intensity of the emotions they experience. All emotions follow a path. There is the moment they experience a reaction that leads to a peak of intensity before the reaction subsides. If the reaction is subtle, don't hesitate sharing what you noticed. If the emotion is intense, silently hold a safe space for them to process the moment until the intensity subsides.

Remember to stay present with your own discomfort. Your brain may trigger a fear response when their emotions erupt. Accept this as normal. The quicker you notice any tension in your body, the faster you can breathe into and release the tension while remembering to feel curious and not judge the experience they are sharing with you.

Stage 4: Confirmation

As you sense their reaction subsiding, ask if they would be willing to share what is on their mind at that moment. Be sure to ask how their realization impacts the desired outcome you agreed to at the start of the session. The answer to your question "What is stopping this capable person from resolving the problem on their own?" may be be revealed.

The safer they feel with you, the more willing they will be to articulate what they see. They may not use full sentences; they might not be able to fully articulate what they see right away. Compassionately reflect whatever key words they use, asking what the words mean to them. As the coaching continues, the insight might even shift a bit as they talk about their new way of seeing the situation and themselves. The lightbulb moment may fully pop into view later, even after the session is over.

BREAKTHROUGH COACHING RESOURCE

Nine Types of Silence

When you choose how to use your silence, you can align with, shift, and possibly transform the thinking of the person you are with, but you must consciously choose how you are holding your stillness. Being quiet is not enough. The texture of your silence matters. The emotions you feel and the regard you have for the person you are with demonstrate if you are open or closed to receiving what they are sharing.

Author and psychotherapist Paul Goodman identified nine kinds of silence in his classic book *Speaking and Language*. Some of these variations can hurt your connection with others more than help it. For example, choosing not to speak as you impatiently wait for your turn to talk can be disruptive. You are not present. They may yield the floor to you, sensing you have something you are anxious to share, or they look away as they talk to avoid your energy.

Here is Goodman's list with slight modifications. You may combine the types of silence you use. Questions and explanations are offered so you can be aware of and choose how to use your silence in coaching at will:

1. *Dumb silence or apathy*—Do you have nothing to say because you don't care? Your response can be out of context because you heard only fragments of what they said or you look for a way to leave the conversation completely.
2. *Sober silence or numbness*—Are you just listening because you feel you have to? You may try to interact, but you feel trapped instead of engaged.

3. *Noisy silence of resentment*—Is the person saying things that conflict with your values or speaking in a way that is so irritating it hurts your ears? You hear only enough to respond with a few words so you don't sound annoyed or bitter.

4. *Baffled silence of confusion*—Are you stuck feeling unsure of the intention of the conversation, the meaning of the words, or the direction the story is going? You are reluctant to say anything because you might sound ignorant or underinformed.

5. *Musical silence that accompanies absorbed activity*—Whether you are alone or with others, are you so immersed in the activity that it feels as if the world doesn't exist around you? This usually happens when you are creating, composing, or playing a sport. It can also happen when engaged in meaningful dialogue.

6. *The silence of peaceful accord, in awe of the beauty of the moment*—When seeing a beautiful sunset or magnificent panorama, do you feel a stunning combination of peace and curiosity? The soul stirs and you are engrossed in pure attention and discovery. You may feel a sense of oneness with the world, opening your heart to love, appreciation, and gratitude. You feel fully alive.

7. *Harmonious participation emerging from your silence*—Do you sense you are in harmony with what is unfolding in your conversation? Observations and questions arise from your curiosity, respect, and care for the person, not from your analytical mind. You are in peaceful accord with the person you are with.

8. *Alive silence with holistic perception*—Are you noticing everything in your visual sphere? Acoustic ecologist Gordon Hempton said, "Silence is not the absence of something but the presence of everything." You want to zoom out instead

of zooming in to details so you can absorb everything that is being offered to you. You don't latch on to one thing but clearly see connections and distractions. This is the opposite of musical silence, where the world around you doesn't exist. Here your awareness is total and all-encompassing.

9. *Appreciative silence when listening*—Does your silence feel like a container, open to taking in the essence of the person's meaning from their words, their expressions, and the energy they radiate? You not only understand their experience but also tenderly reflect what you hear and notice to help the other person assess their thinking. This silence is dynamic, but what you share with the person is not intrusive. This silence is incredibly useful for effective coaching and leadership conversations, and probably parenting as well.

Before coaching, open your mind and body with the silence of peaceful accord. Then during coaching, practice alive, harmonious, and appreciative silence to create safety and connection while receiving what is offered. People will relax into the container you hold, willing to reveal what is on their minds that they do not understand. Your curiosity and care will shepherd a new awareness filled with possibility. Start your practice of silence today.

 **BREAKTHROUGH COACHING EXERCISE**

Coaching Practice: What Are You Listening For?

Practice exploring the meaning clients attribute to their words, the identity they bring to their current situation, and who they would like to be when they realize their desires, the vision of what they would like to create, and the obstacles they perceive are holding them back.

Instructions

One person coaches a volunteer client for no more than twenty minutes. An observer times the conversation, letting the coach know when two minutes are left. When the observer indicates there are two minutes left to wrap up, the coach will end the session by asking the following questions:

1. What do you understand better now?
2. What is the next step you will take?

The coach should review the following guidelines before the session:

1. Start the session by asking what challenge or possibility the client would like to explore.
2. Accept and appreciate the client's perspective of the challenge.
3. When they pause or begin to repeat themselves, ask if you can summarize what you heard them say they want to address or change and why. Once they confirm or alter what you shared, ask questions and summarize responses that do the following:
   - Explore the *meaning* of their words. Identify key words they use to describe the obstacle, what they are feeling, and what they think they need. Remember to ask your questions one at a time; do not combine multiple questions.
   - Explore their vision of what they want instead of what they have now. How would they like this story to end? If everything turned out well, what will have changed?
   - Explore their own identity. Once they describe the challenge or problem, ask who they see themselves being in this situation today. When they clarify the vision of the outcome they want to create, ask what they might change in themselves to feel more content, fulfilled, or successful. Then toward the end when they commit to actions, ask who they will be once they take these actions.

- Explore potential obstacles. What do they need to address or resolve right now to be able to move toward their vision? What beliefs about themselves or others do they see as holding them back? What fears about the future are stopping them from taking any steps? What *shoulds* from family, friends, bosses, or society are confusing their choices?

4. Agree on a desired outcome. Coach them to get a tangible outcome that you can agree to, a picture of what the client wants that is not occurring at that moment. This is not an action, decision, or feeling. What will they have when they act, decide, or feel differently?

Debrief after each coaching session by stopping to answer the following questions:

- Coach: What did you learn by focusing on coaching the client's perspective of the situation and themselves?
- Client: How did the coaching help you identify what you want to create or change, and what you can do to move toward your desires?
- Observers: What did you learn watching the coaching session unfold?

PART THREE

What Is Their Desired Outcome *Really*?

When you are coaching one-on-one, facilitating a team meeting, or trying to listen to an upset friend, one of the most difficult things to do is keep the conversation on track to a fulfilling resolution. It's not that the topic changes, it's that the destination wasn't made clear. When people's outcomes from a conversation are not clear, it can feel as if you are chasing them in circles. You often end up where you started. Either they won't feel confident in the actions they stated they will take, or they say they need time to reflect on the conversation before deciding to do anything different.

Coaching must juxtapose control with flow. You want to have a spontaneous interaction focused on the person's agenda, not yours. You listen and appreciate their story because hearing their perspective without judgment is important. At some point, you must take charge of ensuring the conversation has a destination. You then maintain some sense of control over the direction of the conversation so you stay on track toward the moment when they know what they are willing to do next.

With practice, you can merge control with flow so they always feel safe and respected. The coaching will end with a satisfying sense of progress.

> You allow and control at the same time without leading them where you think they should go.

Remember, you are partnering with them to realize something they are longing for but often resist naming. They might be stuck in the myth that they cannot have what they want, or they fear the burden of claiming a desire that will be judged as impulsive, unachievable, or too risky. The realization they gain through coaching is often a simple awareness that they are worthy and can take at least one step toward what they desire. They see that the step is not precarious but safely within their reach.

The destination must be clarified for the journey to begin. You help paint the picture of what is possible. There may be a change in the landscape on the path forward. Defining the outcome is a cocreative process, where you invite the person to clarify and choose while they see their world in a broader way. You will nudge the person to declare the destination while responding with ease to their level of willingness and the pace they need to process their insights.

You direct this process with both firmness and care. You maintain their feelings of safety and trust as they move through the discomfort of letting go of their story. You sense when the conversation stabilizes as they confirm their desired destination. You gain their permission to dig deeper into what they think is holding them back and what can and cannot be done to clear the way forward. You coach with care even when you bravely challenge their thinking.

The vision of their desired outcome doesn't just call them to act differently; it calls them to step into a new or renewed sense of self as their reality shifts. Robert Biswas-Diener defined coaching as an invitation for coachees to reflect on how they view themselves and the current situation in the context of an "articulated desired future."[1] Coaching who they can become as they move toward a new view of what is possible ensures enduring growth.

The desired outcome is then woven into the conversation as the golden thread that keeps the evolution of the story on one track to the end. Keeping the picture of their desired outcome in mind and acknowledging when it broadens or shifts gives more substance to the steps they declare they will take as you move to closing out the conversation. The entire interaction gives the client the power to drive their future while knowing where they are going and the possible rewards for staying on the path. Their story shifts from feeling stuck under a cloud of confusion or displeasure to feeling the warmth of a strong sense of purpose. Knowing what they will do next to achieve what they conceived inspires them to take charge of their destiny even if they are still afraid.

Defining the desired outcome is both an intellectual and creative process. You don't teach them but consciously help them conceive what can be achieved. Even revealing blocks and executing plans requires that you activate both their logic and imagination.

Sometimes, coaching will feel like a negotiation as they navigate conflicts of values. You want for them to have a meaningful life, but how they define themselves as a good parent, leader, or partner can make them feel selfish if they put themselves first. The negotiated outcome may be the answer to reconciling their desires with the demands of their current life.

They do not have to concede to their social contracts. They can plan to pace themselves as they move toward their desired future with their current responsibilities in mind. Coaching brings this awareness to the surface when their *shoulds* dampen even the act of dreaming.

Coaching to define the outcome is a process of reconnecting with the self. You turn the lens of discovery on their thinking to examine, understand, and use their agency to make their relationships and life journey more satisfying. They reclaim their selves and their powers as they take a stronger stance in making and acting on their decisions.

CHAPTER 9

The Need for a Clear, Observable Desired Outcome

T he picture of the desired outcome provides the framework for the coaching conversation. A clear and inspiring vision provides the stamina needed to break through the hard shell encasing the story that is holding your coachees back. When they have a desired outcome to hold on to, the coaching can more easily dissolve their resistance and open their eyes to a broader view of themselves and the situation they are facing.

Without a clearly defined outcome, coaching stays on the surface with little change in perspective. Coachees may process information when talking about it and may even agree to trying something new, which has value, but no real transformation has occurred. They may make incremental changes in their routine, but old fears and beliefs will likely crop up as saboteurs to sustainable, long-term growth.

To keep a conversation on track to achieving desired shifts in relationships, jobs, life purpose, or one's sense of self, you must first coach the person to clearly state what they truly want. The outcome is not a decision, feeling, or action plan. What will the decision, new feeling, or plan give them? For example, some people will come to the conversation with a goal to make a decision, but the real problem is they have made a decision they are afraid to implement. This often happens when someone wants to leave a job or relationship. The outcome the person wants is not to make a decision or to understand their discomfort but to determine how to navigate the risks for taking the leap they already decided they want to take.

Coaching Case Study

My client started our conversation saying she felt so overwhelmed at work, she woke up with little energy at the start of the day. She said she couldn't do anything right because she had too many priorities that kept piling up. She was afraid she would start making big mistakes and be seen as a failure. Her boss told her she had to learn how to prioritize her work or find a better system for organizing her office. When she mentioned these options, her voice had no energy in it. I told her I didn't sense any excitement for the prioritizing and organizing options she was told to do.

She paused, looked away, and then came back with a voice tinged with anger. She said she was angry about what had happened to her career. She felt her best talents and what she was trained to do were being underutilized. She didn't enjoy the projects she felt were dumped on her. Lost in resentment for her boss and her self-blame for the situation she was in, she struggled with focusing on her work.

If I had accepted the initial options of looking at how to better prioritize or organize her work, the conversation would have been a dull exploration of time management options. Instead, we explored what was expected of her and what she would rather be doing.

She painted the picture of the job she wanted to create for herself that would use her gifts and help her grow. She wanted work that honored her values of learning and tackling new challenges. She needed to feel as if her contribution was making a significant difference to the organization. She didn't need to leave the company, not yet. Instead, she designed a new role, positioning it so she could describe how her strengths and values would best serve the organization.

To her surprise, her boss readily aligned with her request. The next year she led a new venture with renewed motivation. She was still super busy but did not feel weighed down by doing a job she felt was a disappointing dead end.

Dig beyond the Presenting Topic

People are often unsure about what they really want. Breakthrough coaching brings their blocks and desires to the surface, standing them side by side so they can see the whole story and what they want to change and what they need to do to make sure their next chapter is more satisfying and fulfilling. Most coaching starts with coachees giving a convoluted story about what is going on without a clear statement of what is in their power to change. They are thinking in emotion-driven circles. You have to peel away layers of the story so they can clearly see and declare what they want instead of the problem they see.

When the conversation feels as if it isn't going anywhere, dig deeper by asking what they are afraid might happen if they make certain choices or what doubt rises up every time they attempt to imagine a different future.

The clues will be in their story. You start the conversation by asking what challenge they want to explore or topic they want to discuss. Often, they say in their first sentence what they want and then go into a litany of grievances, worst-case scenarios, excuses for inaction, and rationalizations for not trying to achieve what they want.

To bring the conversation back on track, remind them what they said they wanted, such as "You said what you wanted, but you don't think this is possible. Would you like to explore if you could make this happen?" They will often not remember what they said, so use their words to specifically remind them what they declared they wanted to create or change. Then ask what their key words mean, such as *confidence, respect*, and *energized*. You might ask them to say more about the emotions they mentioned, such as *stuck, angry*, or *tired*.

Invite them to consider what life would look like if the obstacles they named didn't exist. The goal is to look at the flip side of what isn't working to imagine what they could create instead. The conversation won't move forward without recognizing how their story could be different in the future. Only then can you have a relevant discussion around what challenges need to be addressed and resolved.

It's possible the person does not have a particular outcome in mind when you begin the conversation. There may be a topic to discuss, such as what to do at business meetings or how to build relationships with peers. You still need to prod the person for at least a preliminary outcome of the conversation, asking questions such as "What will you find easier to do once we explore this topic?" or "I would be happy to explore this topic with you—what made you bring it up with me right now?" Listen for the need or wish that prompted their curiosity.

Coaching Case Study

When starting a recent coaching conversation, my client said her goal was to work with her project team to create a solid action plan everyone would agree to. She sorted through possible approaches. I said, "You seem to have solid options to consider. Do you want to focus on what is standing in the way of you making a decision about what to do, or is there something going on between you and your team that you need to resolve before you present them with your request?"

She hesitated before she said, "I just want them to get their act together and agree to something. The team has split in two. They have taken sides on opposite ends of the spectrum when it comes to what we think we need to do, but neither side is budging. Time is running out. The team might be dissolved if we don't agree on a plan. How do I make them see that?"

Her agitation was palpable. I asked, "How responsible are you for the success of the team?"

"I will look like a lousy leader if I fail. Maybe I am the problem, but they don't report to me, so I can't make them do anything."

"You said they needed to understand the imminent consequences if they don't agree to a plan. Right?"

"Yes, I want them to see and accept the reality."

"And you are judging your value as a leader on your ability to find a way for them to want to work together."

"Yes, I want them to willingly engage in a negotiation. Or at least I want them to declare the stalemate."

"What is stopping you from giving them this ultimatum?"

"I'm afraid of their reaction."

"What reaction do you expect to get?"

"Hmm . . . I guess I'm most worried they will reject me, treat me like I don't know anything. But I do. That's why I was asked to take the lead on this project. I was asked to take charge. I need to do that. I think I need to forcefully tell them the bottom line is they either negotiate or disband the team, opening the door for other people to work on this together."

"It sounds like you don't want to be the facilitator, but you want to be seen as the person in charge. Describe to me who you are when you deliver the message that needs to be heard." She described how she looked, sounded, and felt when she presented her observations and what she needs to ensure will happen next. Then she said she needs to show up in her power no matter their reaction.

Once she could envision stepping into her power, she adamantly declared the steps she would take to activate her strong leadership presence in the next meeting.

The Process of Clarifying and Agreeing on an Outcome

The steps shown in figure 9.1 can help you create the vision and thread that keep the conversation moving forward. You will relate back to what the coachee envisioned as a desired outcome as they talk about what needs to be resolved and what is difficult to change. When they commit to taking steps at the end of the session, ask if they think or feel the steps will move them toward what they desire and what will happen if they hit a pothole in their plan. These statements ensure progress and growth.

Ease into the conversation by asking them what is most pressing on their mind, what they would like to talk through that day, or what has happened since you last spoke. If they present more than one dilemma or topic to explore, recap what they shared and ask what would be most critical for them to resolve first.

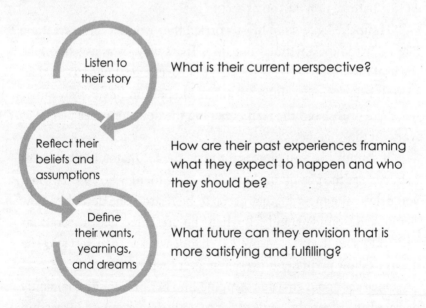

Listen to their story

What is their current perspective?

Reflect their beliefs and assumptions

How are their past experiences framing what they expect to happen and who they should be?

Define their wants, yearnings, and dreams

What future can they envision that is more satisfying and fulfilling?

Figure 9.1. The process of clarifying and agreeing on an outcome

Use the following steps as guidelines for agreeing on an observable, desired outcome:

1. Listen as they unwrap their story. Pull out what is most irritating, confusing, uncomfortable, disappointing, or desirable. Reflect what you hear to agree on what needs to change.
2. Coach to clarify what the person actually wants to create, feel, have, or be different from their current situation. Listen for what they tell you they want but don't believe will happen, what they discount because they fear they will fail or aren't worthy of having. While they tell their stories, listen for the words *really*, *but*, and *should*. Reflect the phrases that follow these words, and then ask what needs to be addressed or resolved to remove these blocks. Help them see behind their words.
3. Coach them to paint the observable picture of what they yearn for that you can both agree on. Don't assume you know what they want until the picture is clear. Ask them what the key words mean to them. Ask them what is important about achieving what they want. Drill down to what they specifically want for themselves or what they have been afraid to declare as their personal desire.

Once you have a clear picture of what they want to create, recognize if they drift into a new or related topic. Remind them of what they agreed they wanted to create and ask if they want to stay focused on that or if something else now feels more important to explore. If they want to change focus, start the process over again so you agree on what their new desired outcome looks like.

It is important to define where you are going, or you will go all over the place!

Common Traps When Coaching for the Desired Outcome

Recall or listen to a recording of a recent coaching session. Note when the session resembled any of the following situations:

- Your coaching session meandered or went in circles with no clear direction.
- You hit on the real issue and desired outcome so late in the session that you had little time left for coaching.
- The conversation stayed transactional, focused on actions the client took and can immediately take but lacking any new insights about the challenge. They may have talked themselves into seeing something new they can do, but the coaching didn't alter their story and who they are or could be in the situation.
- You ran out of time to design actions or at least one clear step forward other than "I'll think about it more."

If any of these situations look familiar, you may have fallen into one of these common coaching traps.

Common Coaching Traps

1. You agree to the dilemma or a vague desire but not the outcome they want to have when they perceive a way to move beyond the problem or gain a new perspective.

2. You identify more than one challenge and then choose what to focus on instead of inviting the client to choose.

3. You lead the client to what you think is right for them to pursue or do next.

4. You move too soon to solve a problem by immediately asking what actions they can take.

5. You don't explore what is making this challenge difficult to resolve on their own—which could lead to a more personal desire they want to achieve.

Here are some tips to help you clarify the desired outcome:

- *Don't get lost in their story or buried under the details*—You want them to share what they see, but it is up to you to grab the key words and emotional expressions, reflect and ask them what the words mean to them, and relate to what they want instead of what they currently have. If they repeat what they said or keep piling on details to their story, interrupt by (1) asking permission and (2) telling them why, such as asking "Can I interrupt you to make sure I know where this conversation is going?"

- *Don't accept what they don't want as an outcome*—What will they have when they get what they want or what does the opposite of what they don't want look like?

- *Don't use generic questions*—When you ask "What do you want by the end of the session?" or "How can we best use our time together?" they may just repeat the problem. Customize your questions using their words and expressions to help them identify a positive resolution to the problem they presented.

- *Don't accept vague desires you can't both see*—Instead of accepting vagueness, get specific. Here are three examples:

1. If they say they want to make a decision or plan, ask, "If you make the right decision or lay out a plan you feel good about, what would you have as a result?"

2. If they say they want to feel something different, such as more confidence when speaking up or taking action, ask what their definition of confidence is or what they want to do differently. Then ask what outcome they hope this shift gives them, such as "If you had the confidence you need to do what you think will make you a better leader (or connect with others better or handle yourself in meetings more powerfully) what would you achieve?" Be sure to ask who they will be when they take on the emotion they want as well as what they will be doing.

3. If they say they want to understand what is going on better, ask, "What would a better understanding give you?"

Then the rest of the session can focus on exploring what is getting in the way of this smart person moving toward what they actually want.

CHAPTER 10

Clarifying Obstacles to Achieving Desires

Once the desired outcome is clear, the core of the coaching session focuses on what needs to be addressed or resolved to create the outcome. You ask what is getting in the way of formulating effective solutions or taking actions. Cutting through the fog of emotions to name and claim the landmines they imagine they may encounter can take more time than discovering how to remove them.

Kahlil Gibran, poet and author of the classic book *The Prophet*, is attributed to saying, "Your living is determined not so much by what happens to you but by the way your mind looks at what happens." How you explain what is happening and what it means to you is fabricated from how your mind defined and judged everything that has happened to you up to now. You coach to expand your coachees' interpretations of what is going on and what is possible going forward. Perception is both limited and flexible.

Clarifying the desired outcome could immediately spark a lightbulb moment on what needs to happen to make it come true. Often it's a simple realization, what I call a *duh moment*, that causes people to wonder why they missed seeing an obvious explanation or solution before. Identifying the desired outcome can create a new understanding that feels simple yet is profound enough to open their eyes to what actions can be taken now. Many people have told me the awareness they gain from coaching is even more significant than the goal they were able to achieve.

Clarifying the outcome could initially bring forth feelings of powerlessness, self-doubt, and confusion. Conflicts feel insurmountable. Failure seems inevitable. Fears others will judge their desire or ability to achieve it are paralyzing. This faltering is heightened by cultural practices and family directives and experiences that weakened their trust in what life can offer. Parker Palmer, author of *On the Brink of Everything*, said we must bring what is in the shadows to light. When we can't embrace the whole of who we are and what we are experiencing, we "imprison the creative energies hidden in our own shadows."[1] Your coachees may feel embarrassed, vulnerable, or wrong when you coach them to say out loud what they most desire; stay with them as they move from dark to light.

Blind spots impact the ability to design an inspirational outcome. They must be brought out of the shadows into the light even when it's uncomfortable to weave longings and personal values into a desired future.

Your job as the coach is to compassionately and courageously reveal blind spots with your targeted reflections and curious questions. The increase in their self-awareness may be uncomfortable, but in the end, they will feel empowered.

The Johari Window as a Metaphor for Coaching

The Johari window, created by psychologists Joseph Luft and Harrington Ingham in 1955, describes four levels of consciousness people have in relationship with themselves and others. Luft and Ingham named their model Johari using a combination of their first names, Joe and Harry. They never copyrighted it because they did not realize how important and timeless the model would be for people worldwide in personal and corporate work.

Let's go through the model, shown in figure 10.1, to better clarify how you can use it to deepen awareness and expand the story so possibilities for what to do next emerge.

Conversations start with the client's perspective of a challenge they are facing or a dilemma they want to resolve (the open or known facts). They see the problem, but they have trouble or avoid looking beyond the problem.

The inability to see beyond the problem on their own is because their view is clouded by gaps in their logic and unrealized beliefs, fears, and assumptions (the blind spots). Or they don't want to face their fears of other people's judgments or their self-doubts that make them feel embarrassed, vulnerable, or wrong (the hidden facts).

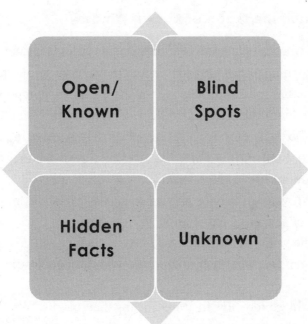

Figure 10.1. The Johari window

If you have created a sense of psychological safety where people don't feel judged, the coaching may cross into the blind spots and hidden areas even when it feels uncomfortable. You use reflective inquiry to explore patterns of thinking and perceptual definitions to recognize beyond what is apparently known. Then the conversation can more readily surface fears and beliefs holding the stories in place.

When the coachee's perspective broadens, a new awareness emerges. They did not have this insight before the coaching session. What they weren't aware of (the unknown) is now known or becoming clear (expanding the open or known facts). What actions and commitments are now possible arise from the unknown when they have a lightbulb moment of insight. This expanded comprehension increases both self-awareness and confidence in the window of what is open and known.

Coaching in the Open or Known Window

This box is what people know *and* they openly let others know too. You start coaching by listening to the story they are telling about why their challenge or indecision exists. They share their current perspective. As you coach them to define the desired outcome, you may go outside the box when they realize old beliefs they are hanging on to (blind spots) or when they share thoughts they have been reluctant to think about before (hidden facts).

Although you are curious about how these revelations relate to their sense of self and what is possible, keep them on track toward clarifying the vision of their desired outcome before you go deeper into understanding what is coming up so you don't get lost in their story.

You might explore how they are labeling their blocks. When they say things such as "I'm a perfectionist, and it's impacting my life and driving my coworkers crazy" or "I worry people will judge that I'm not experienced enough for the role," ask them what *perfectionist* or *enough experience* means to them. Use their definitions to help identify what they want to change in their behaviors and mindset as a part of their outcome.

Coaching in the Blind Spots Window

This box is the most significant area to coach in because people can't access this window on their own. *Blind* refers to what they can't see or know—what they are not aware of about themselves even when it is apparent to others.

The brain's desire to maintain a feeling of safety blocks personal attempts to challenge beliefs and decisions already made. Entry into the blind spots window by self-exploration is stopped by the brain so people have a sense of certainty about daily choices even if their choices don't serve their development. Rationalizing choices is easier than questioning them. Most people will instantly concoct a brilliant reason for procrastinating on a task, for prioritizing reading email over a project deadline, or for making life decisions based on what they predict they will feel in the future when, in truth, no one can be sure how they will feel.

> To open the window to blind spots, we need someone else to summarize our thoughts so we can objectively see them and then ask questions we can't comfortably ask ourselves.

When you summarize what you hear and ask what they think about what they said, you disturb this automatic processing that operates in the background. You use reflective inquiry to open the blinds on the window. Then if you ask them to explain to you how their key words or opinions relate to what they want but think they can't get, you further prompt them to question their beliefs and perspective. You increase their willingness to look into this area as they begin to accept how the importance of acknowledging these blind spots relates to achieving their desired outcome.

With reflective inquiry, they might see the holes in their logic, how their fears are limiting their choices, and how the *shoulds* they are obeying are controlling their actions. Reflections and questions crack the frame around this window, transforming strongly held beliefs into new ideas that lead to actions.

For your coaching to be successful, they must feel safe to explore with you and trust you are working for their highest good. This is why it is important to relax into your curiosity and develop your coaching mindset. They need to believe you are accepting what they share without judgment.

Coaching in the Hidden Facts Window

When people don't act because they think others will judge them or they doubt themselves, they hide what they are thinking or desire. You peak inside this window when they say things such as "I feel like a fraud—they will discover I don't know as much as they expect me to" or "I can't say what is on my mind because my boss will retaliate later or my teammates will sabotage my efforts" or "They will think I'm crazy for wanting to do something else."

Work with coachees to uncover their insecurities. Explore the worst-case scenario if they act in spite of their fears and what else could occur. If the worst-case scenario happened, what would they do next? Will the judgment other people have for them be permanent, or can it change over time? What's the measure of what they could gain against what they could lose? What is the loss if they don't do something? How will inaction impact their happiness and fulfillment? Reassure them that courage is the will to act even when fear exists, and fear is a normal response when moving toward an unknown outcome.

Coaching often fires up their inner fortitude. When the masks fall away and they see who they can be, they realize there is a possibility they will shine in the spotlight sooner than later. At least they accept that life will be easier when they quit thinking what they most desire and value is impossible to create.

Coaching in the Unknown Window

Most of the time, the person you are coaching can't see beyond the fog created by their fear, anger, doubt, or confusion. They are stuck in old thinking patterns they mistake for reality. When you coach them to see who they can be and what they can do beyond their fears, needs, and conflicts of values, the unknown window shrinks. This new awareness is a lightbulb moment of clarity. They now know something new.

By reflecting the key points and themes in their words and the shifts in their emotions, they start to notice repetitive behaviors, recurring thinking patterns, and limiting beliefs holding them back. They begin the process of transformation where aspiring potential becomes personal reality.

Coach them to clearly articulate any insights that emerge. Whenever you see the light in their eyes signifying a new awareness, share what you noticed, then ask one of these questions: "Would you be willing to share what is coming up for you?" "What are you seeing now?" or "What idea just interrupted your thoughts?" Then be quiet and let them think through what is coming from the unknown into the known.

Joe and Harry's Coaching Tool

Thanks to the wisdom of Joe Luft and Harry Ingham, the Johari window can be used as a guide for coaching people how to clarify obstacles so new perspectives come to light. If you are aware of the windows, you are better able to hear, see, and sense what they can't see and what they are afraid to face in themselves as they tell their stories. The blocks to realizing what they actually want as a desired outcome become visible and workable.

BREAKTHROUGH COACHING RESOURCE

Using Closed Questions in Coaching

You may have been taught to never use a closed question and that closed questions are the antithesis of good coaching.

It is true that a closed question can get a closed answer, either a yes or no.

It is also true that sometimes that is what you want the client to do, to choose to say yes or no. When they justify their response, you may ask if they are willing to see beyond what they have been believing so far. When they state an insight, you might summarize the statement and ask if it changes their desired outcome. A closed question can clarify where the conversation is going. The one-word answer is often followed by more words as they articulate what the answer means.

There are at least five situations where closed questions are effective:

- To clarify a client's perception by asking if you correctly understood what they want or need to be resolved
- To affirm if a reflective statement you offered is true for them at that moment
- To facilitate the thinking process when a client has a difficult time articulating an insight by summarizing what you heard and then checking to see if your statement is accurate

- To invite the client to choose what is most important to explore first when they present more than one challenge or desire
- To redirect the conversation when the client changes the subject and you ask them if they want to change the direction or go back to the original focus or outcome

Closed questions are important to acknowledge the direction of the conversation. They can be used to test the validity of a reflective statement. They provide clarity by getting confirmation of thoughts and insights. Even in these situations, clients tend to provide more information, not a one-word answer.

When clients trust you are there to help them achieve something important to them, they will accept the discomfort of an edgy closed question. For example, if a client realizes their actions have been sabotaging their desires, you might ask, "Will you ever be content with the situation as it is?" "Do you want to change this pattern?" "Are you willing to look at what you might change to get what you want?" "Will you regret not taking action a year from now?" or even "Do you know if your expectation is realistic?" Any of these questions can bring to the surface what the client is avoiding. You might follow up these closed questions with an open question about what they want to look at or do next, but the closed question provides the push off the fence.

Quit condemning closed questions. They provoke examination and a forward focus when they are genuine inquiries that arise from your curiosity.

CHAPTER 11

Recognizing Changes to the Outcome as Thinking Evolves

I t is up to you to maintain the direction of the conversation based on the outcome of the session you agreed would be beneficial for them to achieve. You also need to acknowledge when the direction has shifted, such as when an insight led to a new understanding that something is more important or critical to conceive before attempting to achieve anything else.

How do you know if you need to pull them back onto the path or choose to take a different course? You invite them to make the choice.

You must stay absolutely present to catch the shift in direction of what they desire to create. The more significant aspiration can get lost in their rambling about what is wrong and difficult. They might not even hear their declaration of what they actually want because it snuck into their explanations. When I share with my clients what they said they really wanted earlier in their narration, they often say, "I said that?" They are both surprised and happy you heard this statement through their rambling full of incomplete thoughts and distracting ideas.

> Desired outcomes can be blatantly woven and then hidden inside their frustrated rants.

They will often preface the statement with phrases such as "What I really need to do . . ." "I wish I could just . . ." "It will never happen until . . ." "I know what I want but . . ." or "It wasn't what I had hoped it would be." Capture the words they use when they say their wishes, disappointments, yearnings, and unrealized dreams. Ask if these are the greatest desires they want to aim for even if they don't think they can right now.

Reflect their statements and ask questions about their outcomes clearly and succinctly. Don't explain why you are asking the questions. State what they said and ask what it means to them, then give them time to respond. They may be embarrassed about what they had not acknowledged. They may be humbled by the request to consider a longing they never brought to light with words before. Their unspoken desires may have been draining their energy for months or years.

The Invitation to Choose

The session might start with a list of problems they want to talk about. You might summarize the list and ask them what would make the biggest difference for them right now to explore. This is a good start even if something else shows up later. At least you can define a preliminary destination and borders that the route will take so the flow of the conversation has some structure.

Do not zoom in to the first issue they define or their choice of what to talk about. Keep your focus zoomed out in a wide-angle view of the landscape so you don't miss the clues that hint to what they are avoiding or what attachments they are clinging to that are sabotaging their progress.

They might start with what they think is the most important challenge for them in the moment, but a different subject keeps cropping up. You can share the issue that keeps interrupting their thoughts and ask if this topic is more critical to address for them. Then let them choose to shift the focus of the conversation or stay on track to what they initially defined.

If the intrusive side issue frequently appears after the word "but" or "should," it might be a belief they use to confirm why they can't move forward. You might ask if what they said after "but" or "should" indicates a situation that needs to be resolved or a fear that needs to be released before they can envision a more inspiring future. They may say yes, which could change the desired outcome of the conversation. If they say no, the awareness of their immobilizing pattern of thinking may be all they needed to muster the courage to dream.

If your coachees keep backtracking and dwelling on what didn't work before, share this observation. They probably don't realize when they fall backward into fear and resentment. You might even share what they said that sounds like going backward instead of forward. Then ask if they would be willing to step into a vision that is unburdened by past relationships, disrespectful work scenarios, or regrets for not living up to personal standards and promises.

Maybe they need to reimagine an unfulfilling relationship or take what they can learn from a frustrating situation before they can envision what would be more satisfying. If their disappointment or anger is self-directed, ask if the outcome of the session is to discover *who* they would be if they felt differently about their past actions. Invite them to finish the sentence "I wish I could . . . "

When you make an invitation to redirect the conversation, reference the previous outcome you agreed to. Ask if the new outcome incorporates the old one in some way; they could be related to one bigger desire. Say something like "It looks like what you want to focus on now is . . . Before we move forward, I want to make sure we aren't losing anything important about what you previously stated as your desired outcome. How is what you are wanting to realize now related to what we agreed to earlier?" This will help you keep the thread of the conversation intact even when you have a new destination.

The work you do with your coachees to clarify what they actually want to create or become is a significant gift they can't formulate on their own.

BREAKTHROUGH COACHING RESOURCE

Different Ways of Processing Information

Some people think fast and the coaching flows quickly. Sometimes people need to look at all the angles before they feel comfortable articulating what they want or an insight that is coming into view. Understanding the spectrum of how people put mental pieces together to create a new perspective will help you know how fast or slow a person comfortably thinks. How they process information is also an indication that they might react, whether they welcome words that you offer for them to consider or regard your suggestions as an intrusion.

Processing style can be correlated to communication preferences. A number of communication assessments are available for you to use to help you and your clients understand the speed and needs of their thinking. I don't have any recommendations for assessments; use what you feel comfortable talking about when the results indicate a certain style they commonly use at work, home, or both.

For this resource, I will describe these four preferences:

Doers (direct and concise) are quick thinkers. They make connections and decisions quickly and expect others to agree with their perspective. When considering what outcomes to achieve and actions to take, they want what will give them autonomy, freedom, and relevant challenges.

Influencers (relational and talkative) like to think out loud and may change their mind many times when sorting out ideas. They are friendly, enjoy people, and can be creative when considering possibilities. They may need help evaluating if their desired outcomes and action plans are realistic.

Thinkers (critical and analytical) love to gather information. They want to look at all the details before presenting their ideas and may need to mentally rehearse what they are going to say before they share their thoughts. They want their goals to be specific with deadlines and alternatives.

Connectors (nondirect and supportive) count on others to help them determine direction. They do not easily share ideas but like to be asked what they know. They avoid stressful situations but can bend if they understand how taking one step at a time will benefit themselves and others.

Communication preferences correlate with either external (verbal) or internal (mental) processing of information as well.

- *External processors* will think out loud. When they have an idea, they will talk through what it means to the task at hand. They may be organizing their thoughts as they talk but will come to a conclusion only after they talk it through. Doers and influencers tend to be external processors.
- *Internal processors* take their time thinking before they speak. They need your silence and patience. Once they begin to share what is coming up for them, they appreciate when you summarize what you hear and then ask them about the meaning of key words. Give them time to assimilate your reflections and questions. Thinkers and connectors tend to be internal processors.

Here are some tips for coaching ideas into complete and actionable thoughts:

Doers

- Accept their focus on what needs to be changed as an outcome, but be sure you both see the same vision even if they show impatience.
- Ask them to clearly state an insight if their face reveals they just saw something they had not seen before. You may need to ask them to say what they see in one sentence so you can agree on the meaning and significance of the statement.
- Make sure they articulate the exact steps they will take so you both know what might happen next. Their plan becomes their measure of success.
- Don't back down when they resist your questions about how actions will impact others, how reasonable their expectations and timelines are, and what else they need to consider that may have been overlooked.
- Even if they want to end the session, ask them to consider a plan B if what they think will happen doesn't.

Influencers

- Once they describe what they want to change, ask them to state their outcome in one or two sentences.
- Call out any time they backtrack after saying "should," and refer back to the desired outcome to help them accept risking other people's judgment of their decisions.
- Stay friendly. Laugh with them. Acknowledge their emotional shifts.

- Ensure they are satisfied with their stated new awareness or what was most important that they learned from the conversation.
- If they are hesitant about the actions they say they will take, share your observation. Then ask what it will take for them to move forward more confidently.

Thinkers

- Know they will share their thoughts with you when they are ready. Be patient.
- If they jump to actions early in the conversation, ask if they would clarify the outcome they want to create first and what annoyances they might have to deal with when working toward their goals.
- Don't react if it feels as if they are attacking you or your skills. Their inquiries may sound critical, but they could be gathering information about coaching or defending what they fear will be ridiculed.
- Calmly but directly ask them how any insights they share relate to their desired outcome. They may lose track of the outcome they stated earlier in your conversation as they work through the details of their thoughts.

Connectors

- Give them time to talk through how others might react to their ideas and actions and what they will do to stay focused on growth.
- Call out any time they backtrack after saying "but," and refer back to the stated desired outcome to help them overcome self-doubt and fear of failure.

- If they are silent for a long time, ask if they would be willing to share what they are thinking about. When they demonstrate a lack of confidence in changing anything, ask them to share their beliefs about their thoughts so the value of their ideas can be considered in the process.
- Acknowledge their willingness to be vulnerable, and praise their commitment to keep moving forward, especially if they will become a model for others.

CHAPTER 12

Coaching through Resistance

esistance is a catchall word that could be more about what you feel than what your coachees are experiencing. You sense a block that you can't seem to get through with coaching. You could be experiencing their opposition to looking beyond their story, but your reaction could also be feeding their resistance. You may feel irritated with their unwillingness to flow with your coaching. You may fear they are judging you as inadequate and the coaching as a waste of time. The story you make up about why they are not fully engaging with you is your fabricated reason that obstructs your ability to discover what is really going on.

> The reaction you have to their resistance can cause friction between you and your coachee, decreasing their willingness to be coached.

One of the common challenges coaches face is staying calm and curious when coaching people to recognize and talk about any degree of hesitation they are presenting. Hesitation should not be ignored. Resistance will affect the quality of the coaching and the coaching partnership in general.

Shades of Resistance

Resistance is the brain's way of protecting a person from the risks of change. The brain jumps into warrior mode, arming the person from facing perceived losses the changes might generate. The change could be physical, relating to an action they need to take altering their careers or relationships. Or it could be psychological, fearing a required change in self-concept—of who they need to be—that feels uncertain, even dangerous. It is up to you to use your courage and curiosity to seek to understand how they are assessing risks.

Resistance doesn't mean they are uncoachable; few people are totally uncoachable. Resistance can run on a scale from slight hesitation when articulating an insight to deep resentment for being forced to receive coaching. They may be hesitant because they don't yet trust you. Or they may have had an expectation that you would give them advice, not examine their brain. When they blame others for the challenges they face, they may want you to only give them tools and formulas to fix the situation. Maybe they can't imagine a desired outcome that coaching could provide that is strong enough motivation to engage with you.

Let's look at two ends of the resistance spectrum—hesitation and defensiveness.

Hesitation

At the low end of the resistance spectrum is hesitation. This can show up as being silent, looking away, or looking perplexed. After a few moments, ask if coachees would share what is on their mind. They may say there are too many vague details to see a clear way forward. They may think stating an outcome will restrict their options. If you can coach them to state an outcome for the conversation that can be changed, but they still show hesitation, dig deeper into what is getting in the way of their peace of mind. They may not be able to change their situation, but they may discover something occurring now that will help them succeed in the future and gives them hope, energy, or ease.

The hesitation could appear toward the end of the coaching session when they stumble over words or weakly state the next step they will take. Share what you notice, and ask what is keeping them from fully committing to their plan. A new challenge and outcome for coaching might emerge.

If the hesitation appears at the start of the conversation, it may mean that your coachee needs time to trust you. The lack of trust often shows up anytime they say, "I don't know, what do you think?" They are either uncomfortable sharing what they have been considering, or their habit is to avoid the vulnerability that accompanies not knowing the right answer, especially with a stranger. Past experiences or a general distrust of authority, including coaches, can slow the speed of trust.

Review the steps in chapter 2 to help you keep an open mind, heart, and gut to establish and maintain psychological safety. You can also remind them, "I am here for you, for anything you want to explore, not what anyone else wants you to get from the coaching." To melt their distrust, they have to feel you genuinely care about and believe in them. You must believe they are infinitely resourceful when they choose to be. Even the smallest gesture of their willingness to be coached has the potential for great change.

Don't give in to their requests for advice. Remind them that what you would do in a similar situation may not be the best solution for them. Ask them if they would be willing to describe how they perceive the situation so you can at least become aligned with what is important to them and what they need.

Sometimes people just want to be listened to, especially if they feel hurt or are grieving a loss of an expectation, dream, or sense of value. If they push back when you ask questions, saying there are some other things that are important to share, you may listen a while longer before you ask, "What would be most helpful for you right now?"

When I was learning how to coach, I jumped in to practice whenever I could. Sometimes people appreciated my curiosity; sometimes they were clearly annoyed. When a colleague tried to coach me on a situation I was sad about, I shut her down saying, "Stop coaching me. Right now, I just need to be listened to." That experience woke me up to my own intrusions with others.

If you listen patiently as your coachees describe what they are experiencing at that moment, you might hear something that is important to them they would like more of, less of, or to be changed. You might offer them to work on a possible desired outcome that you heard in their story. If you can agree to work on something they desire to achieve, trust and coachability may increase.

If they still resist your coaching, acknowledge that it feels like they just want a sympathetic ear. If they agree, you get to decide how long you want to stay in the conversation. You can offer them a specific amount of time you have to give or explain how coaching could benefit them when they are ready. Do not feel guilty if you don't want to just listen. It will be easier for them to find someone who will listen to them talk than to coach them to go forward.

Responding to "What Would You Do?"

When clients say they don't have an answer to your question and then ask for your suggestion, consider asking one of the following questions:

- "What have you considered and rejected because you think the idea won't work?"

- "What's the risk of making a mistake?"
- "Even if your ideas aren't perfect, what could trying one or two give you?"
- "Do you know someone you could brainstorm with to test out your ideas?"
- "Have they seen others succeed at a similar challenge to yours? What did they do that you could build on?"
- "Have they seen others implement bad ideas that you could use to help formulate what you would do instead?"

You can offer articles or case studies to read that might stimulate their creativity. Giving information is not the same as giving advice. Let your coachees decide what to do with the information you provide.

Defensiveness

Defensiveness is more palpable in a conversation than hesitation but also shows up in varying degrees from "I don't see the value of looking at that topic" to "I absolutely do not want to be coached." In these situations, measure your client's degree of willingness to determine if and how you can proceed.

The willingness to be coached can be developed. Ask if they would share what is triggering any emotions they express as they talk, especially anger or disappointment. They may shut down or open up. It's worth trying.

If they seem to be disappointed, disillusioned, or hurt, listen for how they were devalued or betrayed as they tell their story. Once you reflect what you hear, ask, "Do you want to explore the possibility of creating a different scenario for the future?" You can also ask, "Is there anything you think you need to do to feel complete with your past to create the space for something new?" They may demonstrate some willingness to be in the conversation with you, or not.

If they are resentful, suspicious, or cynical when talking about a past or present situation, ask what promises or expectations were not met that are creating the doubt and bitterness they are feeling now. If they engage by telling you how they were betrayed, ask them if they believe they will always be devalued no matter what they do. Regardless of their response, ask if they would be willing to see if any other reality or situation could have a different result. They may still resist, but you might crack the door open slightly.

If they are unreceptive, scornful, or argumentative, ask if they were told they needed to be coached and they don't want to be there. Ask if there is anything they would be willing to improve or change that would make your time together valuable. Share that you don't want to waste their time or money if they don't want to receive coaching at this time.

If even a hint of willingness appears, start coaching by listening to their story about what is going on in their life that brought them to coaching. Notice these reactions and then ask any of these questions to increase their coachability:

- If they keep wanting to do the same things even though what they are already doing is not working, ask, "Are you willing to find what might work better for you in this situation?"
- If they consistently make excuses for their shortcomings based on external circumstances, ask, "What is in your control to change or create so you don't feel you are on a sinking ship?"
- If they are unwilling to try something new or change what feels uncomfortable, ask, "If now is not a good time to try to create what you desire, what needs to happen for you in the future to feel it's worth taking at least one step forward?"

- If they have lost motivation to change anything, ask, "Is there anything in your life that would feel more meaningful to you, that would motivate you to wake up eager to start your day that we could work toward?"

You might be able to soften their resistance with these questions. If so, coach them to envision a desired outcome that would motivate them to change or activate their courage to let go of old habits and expectations. You need to find the emotional payoff that is strong enough to galvanize their willingness to be coached.

The Courage You Need to Coach through Resistance

It takes courage to coach when you feel the coachee wants to fight or dismiss you. You must create and consistently maintain a safe space for people to ease into coaching or admit they aren't willing to be coached.

Remember to coach slowly; don't react. Receive what people give you in their words, their emotions, and their gestures. Appreciate how they feel. Pause before you share what you notice. Then you can ask what they might want instead of what they have.

Listen for what could be coachable in their story to offer as a possible focus for your time together, or offer to move on when you don't feel like you will come to a mutual understanding. You aren't trying to sell them on coaching; you are seeking the best way forward that serves both of you.

BREAKTHROUGH COACHING RESOURCE

Coachability Index

This following list is a general guide for assessing the level of coachability your client has for discussing a particular topic or for the coaching relationship in general. Not everyone wants to receive coaching; you can't make someone accept what you are offering. Even clients who have been in a relationship with you for a while might still face an issue they don't feel ready to work on. Or maybe your relationship has run its course with no contract deadline; it feels more like a friendship than a professional relationship, and it is time to end the coaching, at least for now.

Remember, clients always set the agenda, not you. Your job is to accept where they are willing to go with you that day and know it could change in the future.

When applying the following list, consider that at levels 1 and 2 there is no opening to develop a relationship. At levels 3 to 6, some or full coaching can take place. From this point, the levels are fluid and can move up or down depending on external circumstances, the avoidance of certain topics, or a shift in the relationship with you. Share when you feel or see a shift up or down the spectrum to determine how to best use coaching at this time.

The Seven Levels of Coachability

The following list is based on the seven levels of coachability developed by the Lore International Institute, a part of KornFerry International.[1]

Level 1: Coaching is not appropriate or ethical—The client presents a psychological or medical problem that is beyond the scope of coaching. Or there is a lack of knowledge or skill to work with, and training or mentoring could be helpful before starting the coaching relationship.

Level 2: Not coachable—The client sees no need or has no desire to change and won't engage in the conversation. The client may show disdain for the coaching process.

Level 3: Very low coachability—The client rationalizes negative perceptions others have expressed and labels their unproductive behavior as incidental. The client resists feedback or won't identify goals where coaching can help.

Level 4: Fair coachability—The client declares a desire to change but does not commit to trying new behaviors. The client shows up for sessions and is beginning to participate in explorations around mental blocks and bigger picture outcomes, demonstrating a gradual willingness to engage in coaching. In a long-term relationship, a wavering motivation could be an indication that the coaching relationship has run its course.

Level 5: Good coachability—An assessment report, request for change, professional or personal rejection, or promotion stipulation served as a wake-up call. The client accepts this valuation and has a new awareness that led to the desire for change. A desirable outcome and coaching goals are easily defined up front. The client may hesitate or have lingering resistance when coaching around emotions, needs, and values. Progress is consistent but might not be instantaneous.

Level 6: Very good coachability—The client requests or accepts coaching to make a change or improvement, either professionally, personally, or both, with an earnest desire to grow. The client has a realistic sense of self but knows a coach can break through frames and boundaries they can't see on their own.

Level 7: Excellent coachability—The client is a lifelong learner and regularly seeks ways to improve. The client appreciates having a thinking partner to help make high-level decisions and evaluate strategies. They may want a long-term relationship with the coach.

BREAKTHROUGH COACHING EXERCISE

From Obstacles to Outcomes

Sometimes it takes a lot of coaching for the client to be willing to define what outcome is possible and desired. This session is intended to give coaches practice being both patient and direct as needed, compassionately listening and knowing when to strategically offer clear invitations to choose or refine the picture.

Instructions

The focus of this exercise is on clarifying the desired outcome within the time frame without ignoring client needs and pushing too quickly for the agreement. The coaching session will be timed for ten minutes with ten minutes debriefing after each session to explore what worked and what was missed or muddled. If present, an observer acts as the timekeeper.

The coach should review these guidelines before starting. After asking the client what challenge or topic they want to explore with you, use these skills to clarify the desired outcome:

- Summarize what you heard. If the client offers more than one problem or topic, invite them to choose which one to focus on first.

- Listen to the client's description of the situation. They may say what they want early in their story—hold on to this statement. When they pause, ask them how the earlier statement relates to what they want as a desired outcome. If they don't say what they want when telling their story, listen for *what they don't want* and see if you can flip it to invite them to consider *what they want* instead.

- Listen for what they believe is stopping them from getting what they want, both external circumstances and internal uncertainties. This is their reality at the moment. Name what you hear, and get confirmation before you ask who they would be and what they would do if the circumstances or their worries didn't exist.

- Clarify any vague terms that can't be seen by both of you. Remember that a verb or feeling is not an outcome. What will they get and who will they be once they make a decision, take the desired action, or feel a more satisfying emotion?

- Notice if the client changes the subject after they say what they want to focus on. Invite the client to choose where to go with the coaching—to stay with the initial agreement or to define a new one.

- Be sure you both agree on what the desired outcome looks like.

Debrief by stopping to answer the following questions after each coaching session:

- Coaches: What did it feel like to keep your client on track toward a desired outcome?
- Client: What was most useful for you in this interaction?
- Observers: What did you learn watching the coaching session unfold?

PART FOUR

Debugging the Operating System

"But this is the way I have always done it" is one of the most common phrases you will hear.

When coachees say they have been acting a certain way as long as they can remember, they are sharing not only a habit but a reason why they probably won't succeed at changing.

When they say, "I will *try* to change," they often mean they don't see a good reason to go to the trouble of changing when they won't succeed anyway. They might even cling to the belief that changing their behavior is a weakness. Changing means giving in. They stubbornly declare they should be accepted for who they are. They are reluctant to admit they are victims of their mental patterns.

Complaints and excuses are windows into the brain's operating system. The brain tirelessly works backstage, focused on keeping life in order, staying as risk-free as possible, and being certain about what is right by its rules. Just as it controls breathing, digestion, and pupil dilation, your brain makes constant minute decisions directing what you say and do based on what has happened in the past. You define the present moment (reality) and how you formulate who you are (identity) using past experiences.

> The mental operating system runs continuously in the background throughout the day and night.

Examining the meaning of habitual phrases and emotional reactions can shine a light on the operating code your brain is using. This inside view helps you understand how your thinking is driving your behavior while activating your ability to see options for future behavior. You gain free will over the automatic operating system.

Yet shining a light on past behaviors can feel unsettling. When you see how destructive or senseless your reasoning has been, you might get angry or embarrassed, feeling like the dumbest person on the planet. Regret might cloud the fact that with this clarity comes the power of choice to think and behave differently.

This is why you can't coach yourself. The brain protects you from feeling stupid and vulnerable. Beyond the obsolete beliefs and gloomy assumptions, there are social needs and life values screaming to be recognized. These bugs in the mental programming keep the system running slow and sometimes freezing up. The wise person knows calling a coach is the best way to expose the elements distorting the operating system.

Debugging the operating system with coaching promotes conscious decisions instead of ceding control to an antiquated autopilot function.

CHAPTER 13

Looking Inside the Operating System

When my computer acts weird in any way, I first try a software program to clean out unwanted files, fix broken registry items, and eliminate malware. If it still is erratic, locking up, or keeping me from completing a task in the way I expected, I call my computer lady who calls herself a *geek*.

Coaches are geeks who can help locate obsolete files, drivers that need updating, broken links, and any other bugs that negatively impact perception. When coachees struggle with making decisions or changing ineffective behaviors, you help them look inside to clear out the blockages nesting in their brains. This scanning for bugs gives them the opportunity to clean up and create the space they need in their minds to expand their assessment of choices.

Looking inside the operating system is often called *vertical coaching*. The conversation dives beneath the surface explanation of the problem to explore thinking patterns and habits inhibiting movement toward a desired outcome. The outcome is the cognitive restructuring of old thinking patterns. A lightbulb moment instantly upgrades the system.

Coaching begins with examining the operating system that currently exists. Both the coach and client look at the programs directing their thoughts, and then seek a shared understanding of why the challenge exists, the meaning of key words and emotional descriptions the coachee uses, and the picture of what the coachee desires instead of what is occurring at the moment. The shared understanding and agreement on the desired outcome provides the transparency needed to uncover the bugs impacting the system.

You might ask about the cultural values and personal rules of fairness and equality playing into the perception of the presenting challenge. What makes other people's behavior right or wrong? How are expectations magnifying fears and creating overwhelming pressure? Coaching starts with revealing and dissecting the reasons and rules controlling behavioral choices and emotional reactions that are painting their definition of reality.

Make sure you ask coachees to define themselves in the situation. They may describe themselves by their role, such as a leader, junior partner, or parent; expected behaviors or tasks; or who they should be, such as a nice guy, team advocate, or responsible guide. How they perceive their identity in relation to the situation could be the key to giving access to the inner workings of the operating system.

> Much of coaching is based on the client's identity. Their definition of self in relation to the situation either supports or inhibits achievement of the desired outcome.

Therefore, their desired outcome needs to include what they want to create and who they see when they look at themselves in the picture they create of their future selves. Who is this person they want to become? How does this person think, act, and feel?

Once they know who they want to be, you can look at how they define who they are that day and the rules holding their identity intact. Their current identity comes with an invisible rule book defining how they think they should behave. Often these rules are getting in the way of changing their behavior. Without knowing the rules they are living by, they don't know if breaking them is okay. They repeat ineffective behaviors and then feel frustrated, confused, and angry.

When the rules are revealed, they can define new rules to live by. They may resist changing the rules when they fear other people's judgment. Their social needs can rise up and block their transformation.

Social needs both support and inhibit transformation. They are developed strengths that have helped the coachee survive and thrive. Needs become bugs in the system when others don't react to the coachee's behavior in a way the coachee thought they should. Coachees resent not being respected, fear failure when order and predictability are disturbed, or doubt themselves when not appreciated. Needs also impact progress when coachees fear their needs will not be met in the future if they change, so they choose to stay stuck and frustrated to avoid pain and failure.

This conflict between *who I am supposed to be* and *who I want to be* can also surface conflicts of values. First, coachees must confidently state what they most value in their lives—the essential components of their daily existence that support them to feel their life is purposeful, pleasing, and complete. They may have to sort out their own conflict of values relating to multiple desires. More often, their decisions are distorted by the values advocated by family, colleagues, work norms, societal rules, and friends imposing what they believe is right and wrong. Conflicts of values stifle coachees from committing to changing anything.

Going deeper into the operating system examines how their persistent needs and compliant values are shaping their identity. Once social needs and conflicts of values are revealed, you can ask any of the following questions:

- "How are the needs you expect to be met defining who you are in this situation?"
- "Who could you become if you let go of expecting that need to be met?"
- "Is the identity you are showing up with supporting or interfering with achieving what you desire?"
- "What values do you feel forced to honor that don't feel important to you?"
- "Is there an imposed value you could release that is impeding the expression of your best self?"

The next two chapters will look more specifically at coaching the strengths and snags of social needs and how to consciously choose what personal core values need to be honored to feel balanced and fulfilled.

 **BREAKTHROUGH COACHING RESOURCE**

Using Archetypes to Expand a Selves Concept

An archetype is a label used to distinguish a specific definition of self, "How I identify who I am in this situation."

Archetypal patterns show up as habitual behavior based on rewarded behaviors in past social situations or behaviors that kept you safe from harm. The patterns create mental models embedded as an identity. We all have situational identities we claim as "my personality" without recognizing they can be modified or changed.

The name we give to an archetype makes it easier to explore how the habitual behaviors are serving or hindering goals in specific situations. Then you can look at other patterns that can be integrated to get better results.

When coaching, you can ask your client, "When looking at the situation, how would you define who you are being? Who else could you be that would get more effective results and still give you a sense of control?" This inquiry gives clients the agency to choose how they want to show up.

For example, early in my career, showing up as the strong Warrior who could fix everything served me well. The companies were in chaos. They hired me for my experience and knowledge around changing organizational cultures. However, as a small woman in a room of large men, I had to have a powerful voice to be heard and respected. It worked, until it didn't. The higher I rose in the companies, the more conflicts I encountered.

In the last company I worked for, we completed a wildly success-ful transition. My boss told me to accept I had earned my new seat at the leadership table, so I could quit pushing people so hard. He then said, "To make this work, instead of forcing people to do what you want, can you inspire them to see what you see?" In the next meeting, I showed up as the inspiring Visionary, an identity I had silenced for years. I liked sharing pictures of what was possible in the future. I enjoyed engaging everyone to talk about how we could make this happen. I had forgotten this part of me. It worked. They began listen-ing to me again.

> Being able to dance with archetypes that feel natu-ral to you gives you control. You take the lead as you choose who to be in any situation. You change both the narrative and the outcome.

When coaching, explore what archetypes your client might use to define their behavior and acknowledge how important these behav-iors were in the past. The patterns could still be useful in the future. Then look at other patterns that could be more effective drivers in current situations. Then ask if changing their archetype is possible if the situation calls for them to make a shift to succeed or be safe.

Ask the following questions when coaching:

- "How do you define yourself in this situation?"
- "How do others respond to your behavior?"
- "Who could you be to better serve the outcome you are hop-ing to achieve?"

We all have at least three dominant archetypes—patterns we typically demonstrate in differing situations. They are authentic ways of being, not roles. Then we have secondary patterns we used in the past but set aside or forgot as we experienced missteps and victories. Secondary selves are still there for us to step into when we remember.

Table 13.1 shows a list of common archetypes I have used with my clients. Descriptions of the archetypes are in appendix A and on the website page covisioning.com/archetype-descriptions-to-discover-your -selves-concept/.

TABLE 13.1 Common Archetypes

Adventurer	Advocate	Artist
Caretaker	Coach	Collaborator
Comedian	Companion	Connector
Detective	Driver	Entertainer
Fixer	Gambler	Healer
Helper	Hero	Idealist
Inspirer	Magician	Martyr
Mentor	Mother/Father	Pioneer
Queen/King	Rebel	Revolutionary
Scholar	Steward	Storyteller
Superstar	Teacher	Thinker
Visionary	Wanderer	Warrior

Ask your clients to take the following steps to create an archetype board of directors so they can see who should be given the lead in the situations planned for the day:

1. Have them choose three archetypes they express most often now, which are their three dominant selves.

2. Encourage them to add two or three archetypes they identify with but forgot about or that need to be developed. What has been held back? What patterns could help them get better results with their current challenges? Add these archetypes to their list of their dominant selves.

3. As a daily practice, they might check in with their archetype board of directors every morning to see which behaviors would reap the best results.

CHAPTER 14

The Strengths and Snags of Social Needs

I laugh to myself whenever I hear someone say, "I don't like needy people." As social animals, we all have needs. Our social needs fuel our drive to make connections with others. We experience success and satisfaction with life when our social needs are met.

Motivation can be defined as the desire to get a need met. Our greatest strengths grow when we repeat the activities that give us joy, contentment, confidence, love, a sense of belonging, and material rewards.

Our greatest strengths also produce our greatest weaknesses. Emotions are triggered when we don't get the reactions we expect when exhibiting our strengths. We may feel angry or frustrated. We might anxiously question our self-worth or feel guilty for what we did wrong. Many challenges presented in a coaching session are fueled by the desire to have a social need satisfied.

The Connection between Social Needs and Success

Children look to their parents and then to their peers to validate their self-worth. Feeling accepted, proud, and loved strengthens the resolve to take risks and achieve. Emotional stability can be a more powerful predictor of success than IQ.[1]

As you mature, you continue to look at people around you as a measure of how you are doing. Their reactions to you affect your self-worth. What you need from others to feel good about yourself becomes ingrained as your social needs. Social needs vary with people based on their life experiences.

Your critical social needs emerged when you discovered what would help you survive and thrive. You found what might help you be seen and appreciated or what will keep you from standing out if that feels unsafe. You learned what you could be good at that makes you feel worthwhile. Typical needs include the desire to feel respected, recognized, valued, liked, independent, and in control.

On the positive side, social needs drive success. My need for attention helps me to succeed as a writer, teacher, and public speaker. My need for recognition drives me to do good work. My need for control helps me take charge of projects and run a successful business.

On the dark side, the rejection or ridicule of social needs diminishes self-worth and confidence. The emotional distress from social disapproval can cause anxiety, self-doubt, and hopelessness. The depth of distress is often related to culture, religious values, and hand-me-down beliefs. In some cultures, parents recognize their children only when they get top grades and win awards. They may punish a child who failed to be at the top tier. When children give their best effort but aren't the best, they never earn the acknowledgment they crave.

Life experiences after childhood may decrease the drive to get social needs met, but few adults ever learned to appreciate themselves. I have coached many successful people who haven't fully developed self-confidence. Their measure of success is based on a less-than, better-than comparison.

Even mentally healthy humans tend to rely on the opinions of others to feel complete.

A self-assured child might grow up less susceptible to the rejection of social needs, but confidence can waver based on situational experiences at any time in life. A generally confident person may avoid risks or procrastinate on tasks that are not failure-proofed. Competent achievers handle success well but not failure. The unknown can rattle anyone's composure.

We tend to seek relationships, careers, and social situations that give us what we need and avoid relationships, careers, and social situations that won't.

Therefore, you are needy. I am needy. Everyone you know is needy. We all want to be seen, be understood, feel cared for, and feel valued for who we are and what we do. We take it personally when our strengths, contributions, or talents are not acknowledged. We feel violated when someone crosses a boundary that impacts our sense of safety, peace, or order. Depending on the situation, our reactions to not getting our needs met range from slight disappointment to rage. Anxiety is often the fear of not getting needs met.

The goal is not to eliminate needs. We coach people to identify needs as both strengths and snags. They shouldn't feel embarrassed by a need; the pursuit of or reliance on needs helped them achieve what feels good or successful to date. Getting their needs met brought them to where they are today.

First we need to identify the value of their strongest social needs. Once the value of a need is recognized, it is easier to talk about ineffective reactions when social needs are not met or when they fear they won't be met. You can remind them that instead of feeling weak and needy, they can find strength from their needs. Remembering how a need has aided their success in the past helps them assess what to do next.

Bringing Social Needs into the Conversation

The impact of social needs on the story used to define a situation cannot be underestimated. The greater the client's need for social connectivity or approval, the greater the needs are intertwined in their decisions. Past rejections and fear of reruns impact willingness and courage.

Don't be afraid to discuss social needs. Bringing them into the conversation won't make clients feel inadequate. Claiming their needs will help them better manage what is in their control to do.

Here are some tips for coaching around social needs:

- *Coach clients to remember the times a need served them to feel confident or safe*—Note that needs are the strengths that helped them survive, thrive, achieve, and connect. Getting their needs met were the motivators that created their current life situations. Which needs are important to them now as their views of growth and success are changing? They have the power to diminish the drive to get a need met that no longer serves their higher self.
- *Make the distinction between who they are and what they need*—Defining who they want to become can weaken or empower the requirement of getting a need met in a particular situation. Maybe their needs for control or to be liked aren't as important as their needs for freedom and significance. They don't have to be subservient to an old need even

when the desire to get the need met shows up unexpectedly. The pursuit of a need should be a conscious choice that correlates with the archetypes they choose to show up as that day.

- *If they have no idea what they need, ask what they would want the other people in their story to say to them—* They might not want to let others think they are needy. Ask, "Hypothetically, if nothing you asked for made you look weak, what might you ask others to acknowledge in you as a strength?" The goal is to surface their important social needs so they are available to explore in the coaching conversation.

Coaching is often focused on discovering the value of meeting or releasing long-held needs on the journey to achieving their desired outcome.

Coaching Case Study

The client was confident she would succeed in her role as vice president of client relations. She had the experience and knowledge to make good decisions.

The challenge she presented was that she felt the members of her leadership team did not have confidence in her. She said her statements were always questioned, and she was always defending her ideas. One of the vice presidents was constantly fact-checking her decisions after the meetings ended.

I asked her how she knew what she shared was valid and thorough. She said she rose to her position because of her need to make a difference. She wants to see her company succeed because of the good work it does. She works hard to make good decisions and results.

I said it sounds as if the others on the team, especially this one colleague who was always fact-checking her work, were not acknowledging the passion she had for getting good results for the company.

She said yes, she didn't need a show of respect; she just needed them to trust her more. We talked about what trusting her more would look like.

Her vision of being engaged in the leadership meetings as competent and knowledgeable became the outcome we would work toward achieving. She agreed and said we could probably use this vision for a few of our sessions.

I asked her what she thought was most important to address first. She said she wanted to talk about the one most annoying colleague. She said she had asked her colleague why he was always checking to see if what she said in the meetings had substance. He said he just wanted to make sure all the details had been considered. His response frustrated her even more.

I summarized what she said: "You don't need him to say good things about you. You want him to trust in the good work you are doing."

She said that was it. She thinks he sees her as self-serving, not being of service.

This was a lightbulb moment for her. I asked her what she needed from her colleague to feel he understood her motivation to make a difference, that she was always thinking of how to best be of service to the company.

Again, she used the word *trust*. She wanted him to trust she knew what she was doing.

I asked if there was a request she would like to make.

She said instead of asking him why he was checking up on her, she wanted to tell him that they had the same desire to make things better at the company, but she felt he didn't trust her.

And I said, "What request might you make to get your need of being trusted met?"

She said, "After I tell him I don't think he trusts me, I'll ask if there is a way we can better collaborate on the big decisions, combining our knowledge to ensure the best result. If he questions something, would he bring it to me first to discuss after the meeting before assuming my ideas are half-baked."

She then said, "Wow, I feel stronger now. It doesn't really matter how he responds, I just need him to know what I think and need."

We ended this part of our session with her commitment to speak with him later that day. I asked if she felt she was moving toward being more engaged in the leadership meetings as competent and knowledgeable. She said this was the perfect way to start.

BREAKTHROUGH COACHING RESOURCE

The Relationship of Social Needs to Emotional Reactions

The strengths that have helped you succeed are also your greatest emotional triggers. Needs stem from times you experienced self-worth and comfort. You then seek to repeat this experience most of your life. When you don't get a need met in a social interaction, you take the offense personally.

When a significant need is disregarded or ridiculed, you react with some form of anger or go inside filled with self-doubt. You may counterattack or stay silent when you don't have the courage to say something about it. Even if you pretend nothing happened, you may never forgive the transgression, further damaging trust in the relationship.

The key is to catch yourself reacting when your emotions are triggered. Then you can determine how best to address what transpired. You might ask for what you need, bringing awareness to the infraction. You might realize no harm was done or that you took the other person's words too personally, and the best you can do is breathe and let go, choosing to feel something else. Be sure your reason for saying nothing isn't a rationalization because you are afraid to ask for what you need.

Table 14.1 includes common emotional triggers, meaning you react when you feel as though you aren't getting or will not get a need that is very important to you:

TABLE 14.1 Common emotional triggers

Be accepted	Be respected	Be liked
Be understood	Be needed	Be given control
Be right	Be treated fairly	Be given attention
Be seen	Experience freedom	Feel in harmony
Experience balance	Maintain order	Be given autonomy
Feel loved	Feel safe	Be included
Have fun	Achieve new goals	Effort is acknowledged
Sense some predictability	Experience consistency	My work is important

Name any other needs you feel you have but are not listed here that trigger your emotions when not met: _____

_____

Some of these needs will be important to you. Others will hold no emotional charge for you. You might recognize a need you don't see on this list. Add what is most important for others to recognize or give you to feel safe, essential, and fulfilled.

Identify three needs you hold most dear. The next time you feel an emotional reaction in your body when interacting with others, ask yourself if your brain thinks you didn't get one of your needs met that you expected to be honored.

When you honestly declare your needs, you can begin to see people's intentions more objectively. From this perspective, you are free to choose what you will say or do next.

CHAPTER 15

The Importance of Values Alignment

L iving in alignment with environmental factors, personal standards, and activities that contribute to your feelings of satisfaction and fulfillment—your core values—creates a strong foundation to walk on each day. What you value as most important will influence your decisions related to your relationships, career, and other activities you engage in. You will also experience disappointment, anxiety, or emptiness if what you most value is out of reach.

Values are more durable than social needs. Life values and social needs may overlap, such as having a need for freedom in social and work environments and also having a value for freedom that must be a part of your life.

> Values are essential for you to instill in your daily life to feel content and happy. Social needs are what you hope others will give you.

How much we want people to meet our needs can fade with experience and age. Core values tend to grow stronger over time.

Your behavior is the manifestation of your values. Other people will recognize your values in how you behave; they see what is most important to you and what you don't care much about. If you say something is important to you, such as relationships, health, or equality, but then don't act in ways that honor these values, people will judge you as insincere. In other words, they know when you are walking your talk. This is why as a coach you need to know your greatest life values. Why you became a coach and what motivates your development will show up in all your business conversations as well as in your coaching.

You might think you value something because you are supposed to and then judge yourself harshly when you don't act in alignment with what you think you are supposed to care about. Life feels more intentional when you release the need to live by inherited, imposed values so you can design a life in accordance with your innate, genuine values.

If you don't value spending time talking, laughing, and listening to people, you probably won't cultivate more than a few deep relationships. That may be enough if you find joy in nature or on solo adventures. If you don't enjoy spending time by yourself figuring out the right words to use that others will understand and learn from you, you probably won't write the book you keep saying is on your to-do list. Then notice what you would rather do with your time instead of forcing yourself to write. If you don't seek out people who work for you to know more about their challenges because you care about them as humans, you might as well skip the leadership classes. You would do better doing good work on your own than leading others.

Inherited values are adopted from parents and society but may not feed your soul. Failure to consider what values are most important to you, not what values you should have, is like starting your car and letting your navigation system choose where to go based on your past choices instead of a new destination.

Distinguishing Values

To truly know what you intrinsically value, you want to first look at what values you grew up with to validate their worth to you today. Start by identifying the values you inherited from your family and social communities. Which values were you raised with, that your parents said were most important, such as achieving awards of status, being well-educated, working hard, accumulating wealth, following religious rules, being independent, or reaching a higher professional status? These accomplishments might represent your strengths because you are good at them. Your strengths may have shaped your life, but the ongoing pursuit of an adopted value can feel more like a burden than a passion.

Jim Taylor suggested in his article "Personal Growth: Your Values, Your Life" that you think about the values reflected in the way you were rewarded or punished.[1] For example, Taylor asked, "Were you rewarded for being highly ranked in your high school class and for winning in sports, or were you rewarded for giving your best effort and for helping others?" You probably made choices where the reward was your parents' love and praise.

Ask the same questions about the values reflected in the social communities you grew up with and live with today—your religion, school, social clubs, and peer groups. What did the people whose opinion you cared about value? What did they applaud or ridicule? Organizational cultures also have values that make you feel like an outsider if you don't comply.

Once you consider what inherited, organizational, and communal values you adopted, ask if how you are living your life today resulted from what others said you should do or from another criterion, such as wanting to belong or avoiding ridicule. Then seek to discover what you are doing today that gives you happiness, a sense of purpose, gratitude, joy, and enthusiasm. What do you look forward to doing? What is important to have in your living space that gives you comfort? Compare what lifts your spirits to what doesn't that is a carryover from the past.

Give yourself time to realize what is most important to you. Pay attention to your emotional state for at least a few days to learn what you wish you had more of in your life. Knowing and living by your core values will improve your ability to coach others to name and honor their values, even when they have been told they should live differently.

The Values Challenge

Conflicts of values are often what keep your coachees stuck. They don't want the choices they make to disappoint people important to them. They fear people they care about will reject or leave them if they choose what they most desire over what others think is best for them.

When coachees declare what they want for themselves but then say, "I can't do this because . . ." you are hearing their conflict of values. Coach them to separate the voices in their head. Ask, "Who is telling you what is right for you?" You might reflect statements made in their story to explore if the voices in their heads are their parents, a significant other, a mentor, one or a group of friends, or even their own doubtful brain. Once you identify whose judgment they fear, ask, "What did they say is right or not right for you to do?" They may have only assumed what others would say. You could explore what their prediction is based on.

If the directives, opinions, or ultimatums are real, ask, "What approval or support do you need from them right now?" This question could lead to freedom, or it could lead to a delay of dreams. If obligations impede movement, ask, "If you need to live by their expectations, if the *shoulds* are important to honor right now, can you see how you might move in the future from living their *shoulds* to be more in alignment with your dreams?" If they can see this possibility, coach them to set a specific timeline for creating a life that incorporates the values they want for themselves.

Maria Popova, author of the thought-stimulating blog *The Marginalian*, quoted her mindfulness teacher asking, "Imagine having only a year left to live, what would you do with it? Then imagine you only had a day left—what would you do with it? Then only an hour—what would you do with it?"[2] Popova's exercise may help a client who struggles with extricating their core values from what they learned was best for them.

The recognition that they have been denying their personal values and made other people's opinions more important than their happiness may spark an emotional reaction ranging from anger to sadness. Remember to use compassionate silence to let them process their thoughts and feelings. As the intensity of their reaction diminishes, you can ask if they would be willing to share what they now see. You can then ask if they now have a different view of their desired outcome or life. Their answers will direct where the coaching goes next.

Deconstructing a conflict of values will most likely change the desired outcome of the coaching session and possibly the bigger picture of a career or life. They may find a way to tell people what is important to them that might bring up a conflict of values or beliefs. Hopefully, the discussion will be respectful if not encouraging. At least the discussion will be informative, giving others an understanding of why your coachee is modifying their plans and direction.

Living Life by Personal Values Takes Courage

Talking about making changes that honor personal values can invigorate or prompt resistance. If coachees fear ridicule or rejection when attempting to follow their dreams, they may refuse to take the risk or lose the gumption to sustain a change they put into motion. They may need time before they feel they can take steps forward, or they may need coaching around courage and confidence. Invite them to choose.

> When coachees say they want to say yes to themselves when they face possibilities of disappointment or being shamed by others, coaching them to muster their courage is one of the greatest gifts of coaching.

If your coachee hesitates when deciding what they want and need, ask them what they will regret not doing a year from now. In my experience, they quickly answer without thinking. They know what they want even when speaking it out loud is difficult.

Once they make a decision to live more in alignment with their core values, they need a clear picture of what they want to create and become to keep them moving forward. What could they use to regularly remind them of what they want? They might journal about their aspirations. If they aren't sure, you can share how others have vision boards, pictures on the refrigerator or bathroom mirror, or quotes stuck on computer monitors. Even a toy or coveted possession can act as motivation to stay on track. Offer the ideas for them to choose from.

At the end of the coaching session, always ask, "What support might help you honor what you are committed to today?" Letting go of habits and what was comfortable can be difficult. Feeling awkward or afraid along the way is normal. Even declaring to others what changes they want to make takes courage. Asking for help is also a courageous, powerful step to take.

Debugging the Brain

Whenever coachees go in circles talking about what is holding them back, shift to talking about who they want to become and then explore social needs and conflicts of values keeping them stuck in who they are being at that moment. The conversation will provide the clarity they need to more confidently move toward the light of their highest aspirations.

BREAKTHROUGH COACHING RESOURCE

Claiming Life Values

Ideally, all coaching goals are in alignment with the client's life values. The desired outcomes of a coaching session should be in alignment with what the client knows is most critical to their happiness, fulfillment, and contentment. It is also important to differentiate what they most want from what others say they should want. Sorting out *shoulds* versus desires will help your clients make decisions based on clear life values.

Clarifying what clients most value will strengthen the framework of your coaching conversations. When they get stuck making decisions or committing to an action, you can remind them what they said was most important to move them forward despite their fears and doubts.

Here are fifteen common life values:

Adventure—Engaging in new experiences and discoveries that may involve risk and testing limits.

Aesthetics—Having the desire for beautiful surroundings, artistic expression, and sensory pleasure.

Balance—Feeling stable and grounded.

Community—Having neighbors, coworkers, or a society who help each other achieve common goals.

Fairness—Respecting everyone's rights and removing prejudice and favoritism in words and actions.

Family—Taking care of and spending time with relatives and close relationships.

Freedom—Being able to make one's own decisions and choices.

Friendship—Having close companionship and ongoing and supportive relationships.

Fun—Loving to do what brings amusement, pleasure, and joy.

Health—Maintaining and enhancing physical well-being.

Inclusion—Welcoming everyone to participate and making them feel they belong.

Learning—Deepening knowledge and expanding perspective for personal growth.

Power—Having the authority to direct events or people, or the means to make things happen.

Prosperity—Flourishing, being well-off, easily obtaining desires, or feeling wealthy or satisfied.

Religion/spirituality—Believing in the divine and an unseen power, living with gratitude and appreciation, or honoring one's faith.

You can find a more complete list of values in appendix B and at covisioning.com/values-to-live-by/.

I recently was introduced to the PEAK Values card deck.[3] The pictures on the cards were helpful for me when choosing my top six values and then prioritizing this list. If you frequently work with values in your coaching, you might consider adding this lovely deck to use with clients.

You might work on identifying your own top five values before using this resource with your clients. Here are questions you can use for yourself as well as with your clients:

1. What used to bring you joy but doesn't feel important anymore?
2. What fills your heart with gratitude and joy today?
3. What are you clinging to that once defined you but now you need to let go of?
4. What do you dream of doing? What do you long to experience or create?
5. What is inside you that wants to be heard or set free? If you listened to this longing, what would you know you have to do?
6. What can you say no to now so you are able to joyfully say yes more often?
7. What do you do that at the end of the day you are most proud of?

Exploring personal priorities that are needed to be happy in this one amazing life is critical to happiness. This awareness can also help determine a satisfying and healthy compromise that honors different values when living and working with others.

BREAKTHROUGH COACHING EXERCISE

Exploring Selves Concepts—*The Who*

A person's identity—how they define themselves in a situation—forms their assumptions, fears, judgments, and ultimately their behavior. Exploring your client's beliefs about who they are in a certain situation or the expectation of who they are supposed to be could uncover what is making the dilemma they present difficult for your client to resolve.

Instead of coaching on actions to take—the what and how—use this session to practice shifting the coaching to exploring who the client can become if they stepped into a different sense of self. Identifying who else they can authentically be in the situation will change what they will do and how they will do it without needing to spend much time on action plans.

Instructions

One person coaches a volunteer client for no more than twenty minutes. An observer times the conversation, letting the coach know when two minutes are left.

The coach should first review the following steps before the session. *Do not* refer to the archetype list during the session; you can review it before you coach. You will explore identities organically, only asking the client to name who they are being if it would be useful.

1. Start the session by asking what challenge or possibility the client would like to explore.
2. Get clarity and agreement on what is frustrating, scaring, or confusing your client.
3. Ask them how they might define who they are in the situation. You might ask them if they could name and describe who they are being, maybe offering an archetype that fits as an example for them to work with.
4. Ask them if they would like to feel and be seen differently than who they are being at that time. Ask them what they need to feel more content, fulfilled, confident, or successful (use the words they defined as their desired state). Ask them what is most important about becoming this person (aligning their vision with their values). Again, see if they can name the behavior or explore possible archetypes they can work with.
5. Coach them to paint a picture of who they want to be in this situation, including what they would be feeling as well as doing.
6. Explore what needs to be addressed or resolved to shift into being the person they see in their ideal picture. What beliefs about themselves or others are holding them back? What fears about the future are stopping them from taking steps? What *shoulds* from family, friends, bosses, or society are confusing their choices?
7. Before closing the session, ask them what they have discovered about themselves in the conversation. Then ask what they are willing to do next.

Debrief after each session, by stopping to answer the following questions:

- Client: What was most useful for you in this interaction? Was there anything that confused or didn't sit well with you?
- Coaches and observers: What did you learn about coaching the client's identity, how they see themselves in a particular scenario and who they can become if they choose to make a shift?

PART FIVE

Turning Insights into Commitments

The goal of a breakthrough is not having the aha insight. The lightbulb moment is the start-up key that drives forward movement. Describing the new awareness opens a passageway that was out of view before. Either just the beginning of a path is visible, or a clear-cut, well-lit road is in plain sight with fewer bumps than imagined. Seeing the way forward is a pivotal moment, but the subsequent decisions of what to do next define the success of the coaching.

The insight could come as they clarify the vision of their desired outcome, when they say what they actually want out loud. Or the lightbulb flashes on when they unravel what they thought were blocks to progress. They recognize how easily they can remove their hurdles. The next steps are clear.

This is the most important moment in coaching. Stating a commitment to act, whether taking one step or carrying out a plan, gives value to the breakthrough.

> The declaration of what they will do after they share their insight is the actual goal of the coaching session.

In her book *Coaching Essentials for Managers*, Sara Canaday said goal achievement is the payoff for investing time and effort to engage in coaching.[1] Declaring and then taking action is the only quantifiable assessment of progress even if the action isn't measurable, such as when they focus their actions on shifting an emotional state or on finding the time to reflect on what is achievable in the current environment. These commitments are important to clarify too. They must make a clear commitment to do something after the session ends.

The process of creating the goals at the end starts early in the session; getting a commitment for action at the end of the session is a result of your focus on achieving an agreement on what the client desires to have or create as a result of your time together. This agreement not only keeps the conversation on track, the actions they commit to at the end of the session must bring them at least one step closer to what they said they wanted as the session outcome. Then, carrying out the stated action after the session ends is the measure of their progress.

Most of coaching focuses on what is hindering a desired change, but people aren't motivated to act differently without making a stated commitment at the end. You aim for a realization that expands the way they think about themselves or the situation. This realization is generally the lightbulb moment that stimulates their willingness to act. Make sure you notice this moment, ask them to state what they see, and then anchor this willingness with questions defining what, how, and when they will act. They decide what to do. The promise is made to themselves.

This final bookend of coaching holds everything together. When they state their new awareness and what they commit to do, also ask how they will overcome any obstacles that could get in the way to increase the likelihood of success. You may also ask who they will be when they take the actions they are committing to no matter what happens as a result. A powerful way to end the session is having them recognize who they are becoming.

CHAPTER 16

Solidifying a New Awareness to Wrap Up the Breakthrough Process

When developing my skills in public speaking, I learned that I needed to practice my speech out loud. No matter how many times I repeated the script in my head, I would stumble over passages and completely forget a paragraph when delivering to a live audience.

When I practiced my speech out loud, I not only improved my memorization but also found gaps in my logic and better ways to connect my ideas so they made more sense. My brain would hear my words the same as if someone else were speaking. Saying the words helped me develop my message.

The phenomenon is true for coaching as well. Ideas are not fully conceived until spoken out loud. Even when clients say, "Okay, I get it now," you want them to say what they got to make sure their thoughts are clear, to understand how their thinking relates to their situation and desired outcome, and to seed what they now perceive into the new story that is unfolding.

What You Do When They See Something New

At any time in the session, when your coachees pause with a slight smile or gasp, or they look away as they go inside their head to consider a thought that popped up, ask if they would share what just came to mind. These reactions indicate an insight is arising. It could be a fact they stuffed away because it was difficult to face. It could be an answer to your question that surprised them when it surged into view. The idea could take their breath away, trigger tears, or drain all emotion from their face.

Don't miss this moment. The thought that is forming is critical to coaching. You need to be still so their cognitive brain can grasp the emerging concept.

I often see coaches run over these moments, more focused on how they are coaching than on what is occurring. No matter what the coachee then says, which usually isn't a fully formed idea, the coach skips backward in the conversation before the lightbulb moment, picking back up where they left off.

> When coachees step into a new world of possibilities based on a startling insight, the coach needs to step into this world with them.

Whether they say something after they experience a breakthrough moment, or you need to ask if they would share what they were thinking about, don't let the conversation retreat. Here are some tips for gently but firmly keeping the conversation moving forward.

- If they go backward to complaining and repeating what they fear after what seemed to be a lightbulb moment, bring them back to the momentary break. Share what shifts you noticed in their speaking, posture, or emotions. Ask them if they could share what came up in their thoughts even if they had only a snippet of an idea that they then suppressed.

- If they say they aren't sure what the insight they had actually means to the bigger picture, or they stumble trying to explain what is coming up for them, ask them to explain the meaning of the words they remember. Valeria Sabater said in an article about the value of speaking our thoughts, "Thinking aloud is a way to facilitate reflection . . . and analyze information."[1] They may need your reflections and questions to help them better understand how their thoughts and emotions contribute to forming their new idea.

- They may not like the truth that emerged. The saying "The truth will set you free, but first it will . . ." has many endings—hurt like hell, scare you to death, put you on a guilt trip, or, as feminist activist Gloria Steinem said, "Piss you off." Any of these reactions may send your client running into the past or an irrelevant direction. If you help them speak the truth out loud, it will weaken the blow to their self-esteem and hope. Ask them what they could recall about the realization they just had, even if it was something they didn't like. Give them a moment to think about it. If they are uncomfortably quiet, remind them that all the information that comes to mind is important to figuring out the best way forward. If they are willing to share even a piece of the unsettling thought, they are likely to move toward self-forgiveness and a constructive plan for what they know they need to do next.

- Don't push for action right away. They may say they know what to do, but you need to be sure you fully comprehend the shift in their thinking and what it means to them before they jump to a conclusion. Say you want to be as clear about their thinking as they seem to be. Ask them to state their insight in one or two sentences. Ask them how the statement is changing their mind. Ask them what they are currently learning about themselves.

Without articulating a clear shift in thinking and understanding, coaching is just a problem-solving exercise. They don't need you to look at past wins and mistakes or future pros and cons. They need you to tease out a new way of perceiving or the courage to take action as you debug their operating system. Exploring what guilt or resentment is blocking their view and the fears making them believe they won't get what they want will help their brains create new associations. You then shepherd the insight into the light where they will confidently declare what is the right action for them to take next.

BREAKTHROUGH COACHING RESOURCE
Tip Sheet for Articulating Insights

A breakthrough can show up as a truth now realized. Clients often say, "Of course, I should have known this all along." They may blurt out the insight and then relate it to what they just discovered is their block or what action they absolutely need to take to move forward. You have to coach them to share this new information in only one or two sentences so the flash of insight leads to subsequent action.

The epiphany can also be overwhelming. Their emotional reaction can impede their speech. They may need a few moments to breathe before they can share what they see at that moment. Don't get lost in their emotions, even if they cry. Don't save them. The reaction will subside if they don't feel embarrassed or judged by you for having an emotional moment.

If you feel they are uncomfortable, softly say, "It's okay, take your time." Once you sense they are breathing more easily, you can ask, "Would you be willing to share what is coming up for you now?"

Yet sometimes, a slight smile, gasp, or look of shock pops up as they suddenly have an answer or a moment of self-awareness. When you ask them what just occurred to them, they stumble, trying to put the realization into words. The door opened, but details are fuzzy.

You may need to coach them to articulate the insight. All views and understandings must be made tangible by being spoken out loud to be integrated and acted on. They cannot fully explore or make plans based on a vague idea. Review the following tips before your next coaching session to remember how to clarify and use a lightbulb moment:

Tips to Crystallize and
Verbalize a New Awareness

- When a lightbulb moment shows up in their facial expression, indicating they just realized something new, ask them to articulate what they are learning, seeing, or beginning to understand. Use silence to allow them to fully experience the moment. Give them all the space they need to grasp what has emerged.

- If they have trouble finding the words, concisely summarize anything they say and offer what you think they mean so they can embellish or correct your words. Being wrong can prompt them to think more deeply about their thoughts and feelings.

- Help organize their thoughts by asking questions meant to clarify the meaning of their main points. You might ask them to step back to see what is emerging with a wide-angle view. What are they now seeing on the big screen? Is there a message being written? Is there a long-forgotten memory? The big-picture view can help them rise above murky details.

- Accept their response. Don't push. They may not be ready to fully talk about what is coming into view. What they are learning will come into focus in time.

Insights could lead to defining a new outcome to achieve or motivate them to take action. Clarity leads to conscious choice.

CHAPTER 17

Aligning Insights with Commitments

A new awareness could be a surprising and profound under-standing—or not. More often, the aha thought is a "Duh, I should know this" statement. The coachee was so mired in their beliefs about what they should and could not do, so glued to their old requirements of happiness and so sure the worst would happen that they couldn't see the simple idea that would lift them out of the mud.

Knowing what they should do now may be obvious. Be careful. You still need to coach them to articulate what they know now and what they are willing to do.

They may be embarrassed when discovering the solution is so simple. They may call themselves stupid. They may feel angry or sad that they didn't do the right thing before. Don't tell them it's okay; ask what their anger or sadness is telling them to do. All emotions are integral to fueling the motivation to act differently if they are exam-ined, not pushed away.

Hopefully, they will shift to laughing at their all-too-human behavior. Then you can acknowledge that simple, plain truths lead to profound leaps in personal growth and satisfaction.

Coaching Case Study

The coachee wanted to be coached on her increasing irritation with other people's behavior in public. She had always been disgusted by what she judged as impolite and disrespectful actions. She feared her irritation was growing into rage.

We explored what characterized impolite and disrespectful actions and who was being insulted or disrespected by the behavior she was judging. She said she knew she was taking things too personally but felt she couldn't stop being so angry.

We then looked at what she felt was good about her behavior. She said someone had to say something. She might be the only one who had the courage to stick up for others who might be the brunt of rude behavior. She said there is a right way to be in a world where we have to live together.

I asked her how important it was to her to carry the flag for all mankind. She laughed but said she didn't think she could put the flag down even though her dislike of her own reactions was growing.

I acknowledged her ability to speak up was a talent that thankfully had not created harmful retaliation other than name-calling. She combined courage with her passion. Then I asked her if she was willing to sometimes act differently, when she discerned that her reaction would not change anything, knowing other times her words would have the impact she hoped to make.

She said that she needed to both calm down and be more selective when speaking up.

I said, "I'm sure you have known this is what you need to do for a long time, but you haven't done it, right?" She confessed to her resistance to change. I said, "When you see yourself being calm and speaking up more selectively, who are you being that isn't showing up today?"

After a long pause, she said, "Compassion in action." She went on to describe how tolerance, and even having the courage to care about people doing thoughtless things, would be the person she could appreciate.

I recognized her affirmation by saying, "There seemed to be both strength and sorrow in your insight. Can you tell me your experience when the words *compassion in action* came through for you?"

She shared that it felt she wasn't letting herself be this person before, which made her feel sad but convinced she could be this person if she let herself commit to the change.

I asked her if being more tolerant and caring would be a new experience for her. She quickly said, "No. That's the crazy part about this. I do it when working every day. It's my job!"

I stayed silent. She finally said, "Oh, it's that simple. Of course." I asked what "that simple" meant to her. She said, "Of course I can be more tolerant and caring, even at the grocery store." She then described what she would do to stay in alignment with the part of herself she most admires at work in all environments; most importantly, she said she would work on being more present than reactive so she could shift her emotions to be more tolerant and caring when she felt her anger bubble up.

I asked if anything could get in the way of doing what she desires. She said she would need to practice. She added with a smile, "I won't be perfect." She said she would journal the steps she was taking and focus on the times her shifting worked to prove to herself she was improving.

I moved to close the session by asking if she had achieved her desired outcome to react more calmly to thoughtless behavior. She said yes and that it felt like she had been holding her breath for a long time, until now. We both released a big sigh and then sweetly laughed together as two humans before closing the session.

Breakthroughs Are Normal, Not Elusive

The limiting belief that breakthroughs rarely happen will lead you to focusing more on the actions your client should take instead of exploring what has been holding them back. Exploring can include looking at *who* is holding them back. If they were watching themselves in a movie, how would they define the person in the scene, and how does this identity drive their behavior? What beliefs and social needs seem to be guiding the character's choices? Then bring the coachee back into the moment, asking how the person in the movie differs from the person they want to be. What would they like to do less and more of? What direction do they want to take next? What identity do they want to develop that feels more satisfying and fulfilling? Even small shifts in perspective can be considered breakthroughs if they lead to new behavior.

A breakthrough that reshapes your client's story is *always* possible.

The awareness is often the solution they have been unconsciously avoiding but is sitting just below the surface of conscious awareness. Their brain is protecting what they rationalize as right because being wrong is uncomfortable. The breakthrough comes when the reflection you make and question you ask breaks through the armor the brain has put up.

Stay silent and breathe while they string their thoughts into an idea. Then you can coach them to concisely declare their realization before moving on.

An Awareness Opens the Door;
They Must Commit to Walking through It

Insights sometimes lead to new outcomes to achieve, but often they lead straight to actions. The moment of clarity often reveals the best action to take next.

Don't just let your client say, "Okay, I know what to do." Ask them to state the actions. Both of you have to see the steps they will take to walk through the door that opened.

Then ask, "When you see yourself doing these things, how do you define who you are now?" They need to see themselves fully in the future they are envisioning. Identifying this shift in identity takes the actions out of just *doing things* differently into the sense of *being* differently. You are coaching them to be more, not just do more, than what they thought was possible at the start of the session.

You also need to relate the insight and actions to the agreement you made about the desired outcome they said they wanted to achieve. How do the insights and actions relate to achieving their desired outcome? Are they more confident they can achieve what they want? The actions they commit to must relate to their first or evolved desired outcome so they remember what is important when the new behaviors they will be trying out feel awkward. The desired outcome becomes the purpose for change; they will hold up the picture of what they are working to create as inspiration for sticking with their goals when unexpected events test their commitment.

When looking at what could happen that could cause delays in achieving their desired outcome, ask them what they will do if the change they are creating isn't perfect. Talking about a plan B will not be discouraging. Looking at how to handle setbacks should increase confidence. If their actions are intended to change a long-standing habit, some days their practice will be successful; other days will feel like they are failing. If you don't ask them how they will deal with difficulties, they will feel angry or lose hope when they disappoint themselves. Remind them they might not instantly change; shifting habits takes time. Asking them how they will address the missteps that will happen is an important part of supporting their growth.

BREAKTHROUGH COACHING RESOURCE

Exploring a Fear of Failure

No matter how confidently your client expressed their new awareness, they may still hesitate when they declare the actions they will take. When explored, you might uncover a deep-rooted fear of failure. They often mislabel their fear, saying they suffer from imposter syndrome. The term has become generic for the fear of not being good enough in both their judgment of themselves and in the eyes of others.

Calling their experience a syndrome is like saying they have a disease that can't be cured. A syndrome indicates a persistent pathological pattern of behavior. Instead of accepting this diagnosis, explore how they might set up and achieve realistic measures of success over time.

When the possibility of complete success is vague, the brain resists facing failure by setting up the expectation that the outcome won't be very good instead of thinking things will turn out all right no matter what. A certain level of self-doubt can motivate hard work. Too much doubt can lead to working too hard to prove value or not trying in the first place.

Labeling the fear as *imposter syndrome* can prevent them from growing. Coach them to reframe how they see themselves when they aren't sure of exactly how things will turn out.

When faced with a task that will test their abilities, ask any of the following questions that relate to both possible losses and gains:

- "If you make a mistake, what is likely to happen? If this happens, what could you do next?"

- "What is the likelihood you will crash and burn if you don't perform perfectly compared to the chance you will learn how to fly?"
- "How can the times you don't perform as you had hoped support your learning, growth, and the affirmation of your strengths?"
- "What else can you feel in this moment other than fear?"
- "Can you feel good or excited about what could happen?"
- "Are you grateful for the opportunity? Gratitude can inspire the courage to act despite your fear."

Hopefully, the answers to these questions will overshadow their fear of failure.

You might also explore the following four archetypal patterns that could feed into a feeling of never being good enough. These four patterns often lead to strong performances and high achievement, bolstering feelings of power and success. These also have a shadow side, sabotaging and derailing long-term desires:

The Expert expects to know everything quickly. There is no place for mistakes and being wrong even when new to a role or task.

The Lone Wolf believes work must be accomplished alone and will resist asking for help. Mistakes are inevitable when not understanding the importance of engaging with a group to get the big picture or the details of an ongoing project.

The Superperson feels the need to excel at every role and task they face. Mistakes may be made, but they feel their performance must outshine anyone else who has worn their shoes before.

The Perfectionist sets impossibly high personal standards and thinks everyone else expects them to deliver impeccable results.

Explore these possible behavior patterns with hesitant clients. If they see themselves in one of these patterns, first ask them what benefits they have gained from owning this identity. Then explore the consequences.

You can remind them that the successes they have had can increase doubts when facing the unknown. They want to be sure of success; they have had little experience admitting they can't see the best way forward. This is a common phenomenon with high achievers who become less risk averse over time. They leave jobs with the excuse of boredom or inadequate pay when they were actually given a task they thought was impossible to do well. That doesn't make them imposters. It often means they are committed to doing good work, so they hesitate when they think they won't be able to shine.

Coach your clients to reframe how they might use their strengths and emotions to increase trust in themselves that their best effort will be good enough—if not stellar. Discuss the distinction between repeating good performances and expanding their ability to succeed with learning. Explore times in their lives they rose up in spite of a bad decision. Help them realize the benefits of the strengths they have so keenly developed. They can thrive in difficult times; they might make mistakes, but they won't fail if they choose to stay on the path.

CHAPTER 18

The Measure of Value in Coaching

The power of coaching rests in how the session is completed. A strong ending not only confirms action will be taken, it also ensures sustainable change over time. The ending reinforces both confidence and the resolve to grow.

How you end the session not only builds their confidence to take the next step but also to know what to do when what occurs doesn't look like what they imagined. They see themselves in the bigger picture as creators, not victims.

> The ending ensures the humans you are coaching see how the current conversation gives them both solutions and a view of what is possible in their overall journey.

In the simplest view, wrapping up the coaching session with the coachee verbalizing a commitment to action provides a way to measure progress for both the current conversation and the goals agreed to at the start of the coaching relationship. You don't have anything tangible to evaluate if progress has occurred from session to session without identifying an observable action they take each time you meet. They may even forget what brilliant insight they had during a session if they don't plan to use what they perceived to move forward.

Knowing doesn't automatically translate to doing. "I know what to do, I'm just not doing it" is a common phrase easily supported by excuses. Without declaring a commitment to take at least one concrete step and exploring what to do if something gets in the way of carrying out this step, knowing can cause more guilt than satisfaction.

The stated commitment at the end of a coaching session is more than a goal. Coachees should define an observable action that relates to the desired outcome and can be achieved by a specified date. What makes the commitment more than a goal is your asking them who they are becoming or how they will define themselves in their role or new state of being when they take the action. The recognition of their personal development helps solidify conviction, satisfaction, and hope. Exploring what they will do if they can't carry out their plans as they had hoped reinforces their confidence instead of setting them up for failure. The end of the coaching is more than creating an action plan. The end is the demonstration of the power of the thought-provoking and creative process that defines the coaching partnership. Coachees recognize they are creative, resourceful, and whole.

When you recognize a shift in their energy that could be excitement, determination, acceptance, or even hesitation, offer what you see and ask how they define what they are experiencing. Don't just accept their agreement with your observation that, yes, they feel calmer and more confident or apprehensive but willing, if that is what you noticed. Ask them to describe for themselves what is going on in their body and mind.

If they show hesitation by saying they will try or their expressions demonstrate they aren't sure about what they are saying, you might explore what is prompting their doubts, which could lead to the discussions suggested in the resource for chapter 17, "Exploring a Fear of Failure." If their hesitation isn't fueled by fear, is there something that is tugging at them to go in a different direction? If they say no, worrying that something won't work is their habit, but they genuinely want to commit, ask what will happen if their plan doesn't work. I once had a client who was ready to end what felt like a great session until he said, "Yes, I have a plan, but it could be a waste of time. It's not likely my employee will change, no matter what I say." I asked if his plan is not workable, what action does he need to take? This led to the more difficult conversation he would now commit to having. Coaching is not a waste of time if you ask coachees how they will handle a disappointment or a hijacking surprise. If the worst does happen, what's next? What causes worry rarely happens, but angst subsides and confidence increases if possible derailers are named.

Even if they acknowledge their plans might not work as planned, ask who they will be as they take the steps they agreed to anyway. Imagining who they can be even when they aren't perfect or people don't react as they hope helps to close the session on a high note. The measure of success is based on their improvement, not on others' emotional reactions. Your coachees may not gain everything they want, but they won't lose themselves in the process.

Invite Them to Cross the Threshold

Once they have a new awareness that relates to achieving their desired outcome, turn their insights into action with these questions. They don't need to be asked in this order or with these exact words. You might not need to ask them all. Customize the questions so they feel right for the coaching session you are completing.

1. "What is possible for you now?"
2. "What will you do to create the best possible outcome?" If they go into a long explanation, ask them to summarize each step. Don't summarize for them. Asking clients to summarize their steps helps to affirm their agreement to act.
3. "When you see yourself taking action, how would you define who you are being?"
4. "How will these actions help you achieve your desired outcome (state what you agreed to), or has what you desire to create changed?"
5. "When will you take the first step?"
6. "What could happen that you didn't plan for that could get in the way of you taking these steps?"
7. "What will you do if the reactions to the steps you will take are not what you expect?"
8. "What will you do if you forget your intention or give in to your fear or the comfort of your old habit?"
9. "What could support your development at this point?"
10. "Is there anything on your mind that doesn't feel complete in this moment?"

What If They Aren't Ready to Plan?

Sometimes coachees will say they need time to think about the conversation. They aren't sure what their discoveries mean to who they are and what path they need to be on at this moment. Maybe they have some decisions to consider first. Maybe their discovery about their mental saboteurs is so overwhelming they need time to think about how the new awareness impacts their view of the past, present, and future.

Taking time to think is still a concrete action. They need to verbally commit to an observable action to ensure they will take this step forward. You won't ask all the same questions named before, but consider how you might pose these inquiries:

1. "Can you describe what you are hoping to sort out when you take this time to think?"
2. "How much time would you like to give yourself to do this reflection?"
3. "When can you carve out this undisturbed time?"
4. "Is there anything that could get in the way of you honoring this promise?"
5. "Are there resources that would support what you are learning about yourself?"

Whether they have a full action plan or the simple desire to think about something, don't judge the choices they make. You may want more for them, but it is better to keep your opinions to yourself. Let them walk on their own.

Because you are coaching their thinking, the impact of coaching never ends. The conversation will come to their mind many times in the next few days and possibly forever.

Do They Need a Final Word of Advice?

Can you give your clients a suggestion or your admiration of the decisions they made at the end of the coaching session? Yes, but they probably don't need it.

Don't ever offer something that sounds like a *should*, even if you say, "Based on my experience, there's one thing I think will be helpful for you." It doesn't matter if you are just trying to help. The message is that they should do what you suggest without giving them a choice. They will probably say thank you so as not to hurt your feelings.

The judgment that drives advice-giving is a typical mental habit. You assume they need one more thing to succeed.

I recently had a mentor say to me at the end of the session, "Remember to keep an open mind." She didn't have malicious intent, but I felt the comment was condescending. I am not a naïve child; I didn't need this wise counsel. The statement made me angry. The session ended on a flat, not encouraging, note.

If you think there is a bit of information *they do not already know* and that could help them succeed with the steps they committed to take, you can ask, "Can I share something I learned that could help that you can consider using or not?" Notice if their reaction is inviting or reluctantly submissive. Get their sincere invitation for your comment or release your need to share your wisdom by saying, "I see you have got this. Are you ready to move on?"

To release the urge to tell people what they should do, you have to catch your impulse in the moment. Then activate the courage to let go. You choose to let go of being the expert or helper in order to stay in the role of the coach.

Overriding the inclination to help is not easy. It will take me a lifetime to fully let go of my habit of helping. I may not totally overcome the urge to tell, but I know I get better each year.

Start today. Catch and quiet your need to be useful in all your conversations unless the invitation to share your knowledge is clearly needed. Deliberately practice this even when it feels uncomfortable. Then forgive yourself for being human as you watch yourself getting better at coaching instead of helping over time.

Place the Final Bookend

End by acknowledging the work the client did no matter their level of sharing. If they showed up and engaged with you, they demonstrated some willingness to explore a challenge they are facing. Thank them for staying in the conversation. If they opened up as the conversation ensued, thank them for their willingness to be open with you even when the outcome wasn't clear.

You might ask them to recap what they experienced in your time together. Don't do the recapping for them. Let them recognize what occurred.

If this is an ongoing relationship, acknowledge the progress they have made. Appreciate them for sticking with coaching even when they are busy.

Support their commitment to act even if only one step. Acknowledge the value of their plan and your belief they will have a good outcome whatever transpires from this point forward.

Before ending the session, ask the client if there is anything else they need to say or talk about. If not, ask if they feel complete and ready to end the session. Then either set the time for your next session or just say, "Thank you," with genuine gratitude for the opportunity to be their coach.

BREAKTHROUGH COACHING RESOURCE

Checklist for Rebooting Your Empathy

You were born with the capacity for empathy—to sense and assess what other people are feeling.

As you age, you may silence your empathy when other people's emotions make you feel uncomfortable or when your own urge to make them feel better gets in your way of understanding their experience.

To be a good coach, you need to regularly reboot your empathy. You don't just use empathy when working toward a shared understanding of your client's story. You need to notice shifts in their emotions and energy even as you close the session. You need to witness all their shifts, including when they relax into their new awareness, are eager to apply what they discovered, or hesitate toward the end as if their words made them think about something else but maybe they shouldn't bring it up. You don't need to make them feel better. You shouldn't worry that your questions will feel insensitive. If you stay compassionately curious while you seek to understand their perceptions and reactions, they will trust your intention is for their growth.

Know the Purpose for Your Empathy Reboot

Know why you want to improve empathy. What outcome are you hoping to realize? The reboot won't work if your intention is more self-serving than other-serving. Is your intention to demonstrate you are intuitive or highly sensitive? If you are honest, you may have these desires, but are you also driven by a desire for developing others, increasing their self-awareness, and helping them better understand what they are experiencing? You will better hear what your heart and gut are telling you if you remind yourself before the session that you are there to serve your client more than to meet your needs for appreciation or admiration.

Honestly declare your intentions for boosting empathy. Look at what you say after the words "I want" and "for clients." How do you genuinely feel about the phrases you use? Your intentions should ring true for you.

Practices for Rebooting Your Empathy

Select the activities you want to schedule:

- Watch movies where people must deal with the unfairness of life, such as inequalities, discrimination, racism, physical or mental disabilities or illnesses, family restrictions, isolation, rejection, poverty, violence, and having to let go of and grieve people, things, or dreams. Some stories have happy endings while others don't. Allow yourself to take in people's pain, sadness, anger, denial, and fears to understand their experiences, knowing you can't fix them. Then breathe and release their anguish so you can stay present to the unfolding story. Don't hold on to their emotions. Understand them as best you can as you watch the movie, and practice breathing the feelings out of your body and mind so you don't get stuck in their experience.
- Read fiction the same way as suggested to watch movies.
- Do quiet (sitting) or active (walking) meditations just noticing what is happening right now. When you exercise, feel your body while you move.

- When you are uncertain about a decision, listen to your heart and gut to sense if there is a strong pull to trust a direction. Is there something inside you that knows what to do that your brain is trying to quiet? This is good practice for listening with your heart and gut when coaching.
- Practice reflective listening in all your conversations where you share what you hear and notice while staying compassionately curious without having to offer advice.
- Take an acting class where you feel comfortable playing different roles without knowing all the words. It can be semiscripted or improvisational acting (comedy or scenario playing).
- Notice when your judgment of others triggers your stress, fear, or anger. Breathe and release the tension in your body so you can stay open to listening and understanding their experience.
- If you are able to travel in your own country and beyond, experience other cultures with an open, curious mind.

When you practice, forgive yourself when you drift away so you won't give up practicing every day.

 **BREAKTHROUGH COACHING EXERCISE**

Coaching Insights into Actions

Although presence and maintaining a spontaneous interaction are critical to good coaching, the coach must be mindful of the bookends of a coaching session and the thread that keeps them connected to maintain a framework. At the same time, the coach must be mindful of any lightbulb moments that appear during the session, asking clients to speak their thoughts out loud, explore how these ideas inform or change their desired outcome for the session, and ensure the insights are incorporated in the actions before ending the session.

Instructions

This exercise is best done in groups of three to five people, but two people will work without an observer. Each person will coach for twenty to thirty minutes with the intention of bringing the session to completion. The coach should review the following list before the session. The list can then be used after the session during the debrief.

After the client tells the story they hold about their situation, the coach will do the following:

1. Summarize what you heard. If there is more than one path to take, invite the client to choose the most important topic to explore.

2. Clarify what the client wants to create or shift as the desired outcome of the session.

3. As the session progresses, notice if the client changes the subject. If something else seems to be emerging, invite the client to choose to either return to the initial outcome they envisioned or to focus on creating something else that now seems more significant.

4. When the client has an insight, coach them to articulate what they realized. Ask how this relates to what they said they wanted to create or if what they now see changes their desired outcome. If the insight was a self-realization, ask if they would like to explore how their self-awareness is changing their perspective on what they want to achieve.

5. Ask them to state at least one next step, even if it is to take time to reflect on what occurred in the coaching. Ask them when they will take the step, if anything could get in the way, what they will do if they don't get the reaction they hope for, and if there is anything or anyone who could help them have a successful experience.

6. End the session acknowledging their willingness, progress, and commitment to their growth.

Debrief after each coaching session. Stop and answer the following questions for ten minutes. Use the previous instructions as a discussion guide if needed.

- Coaches: What felt right about your coaching?
- Client: What was most significant for you during the conversation?
- Observer(s): What did you learn watching the coaching session unfold?

What Does the Future of Coaching Look Like?

Coaching has formalized development conversations that shift the responsibility of the discoveries and actions to the person being coached, the alternative to telling or insinuating what is best for them to do. The impact on changing the way someone thinks through dialogue is so profound, conversations that at least start with a coaching approach will continue to be important wherever there is a desire to grow people's minds and their independent agency.

The profession of coaching is also projected to grow. Each year, thousands of people enroll in coaching schools and join professional coaching associations around the world. The acceleration of global changes that affect how we live and the corresponding need to help each other navigate uncertainty will continue to drive the demand for coaches in all aspects and phases of life.

The trends often listed include the following types and aspects of coaching:

- Team coaching is the fastest growing application of coaching as more work is being done collaboratively and more innovative ideas are conceived in activities with teams than during individual contemplation.

- Group coaching for people with similar roles or challenges is also expanding to give more people access to the technology of coaching and the rewards that come from expanding the way they think.

- The requirement for thorough and substantiated training and internationally recognized coaching certifications will increase. Training programs will need to teach people how to coach well in face-to-face and remote formats. Training will include using the energy of presence, accessing somatic awareness and intuition, and embodying a coaching mindset as well as foundational and advanced skills in reflective inquiry.

- Mentoring of coaches and developing coach trainers will increase with the growing demand for quality coach training programs and certification requirements.

- As the means for engaging and retaining employees continues to evolve, entities around the world will seek to develop coaching cultures, including governments, academic institutions, international as well as local businesses, and nonprofit organizations. The initiatives will include certifying internal pools of coaches and teaching leaders how to use coaching skills in their development, performance, and problem-solving conversations with both individuals and teams.

- Ongoing training and development for leaders and coaches will emphasize emotional and social intelligence, mindfulness practices, communication awareness and adaptation skills, and the use of ongoing discoveries in the neuroscience of learning.

- To ensure the return on investment of coaching in organizations, there will be an increase in the use of data and analytics to measure progress and the effectiveness of coaching.

- Discoveries in technology, including AI, will be woven into coaching practices to support coaching implementation and accessibility.

More trends will undoubtedly emerge over time. All point to the longevity of coaching. I remember the founder of my coaching school telling us in 1995 that coaching will go away as it was embedded in different professions and skill sets. It is my pleasure to say he was wrong.

BREAKTHROUGH COACHING RESOURCE

How to Showcase the Value of Coaching

This tip sheet will help you explain coaching to potential clients, unlock opportunities, and set clear expectations with new clients at the start of the relationship.

Successful sales professionals know that sharing the benefits of a product or service is more important than describing the details of pieces and parts. People want to know what you can do for them and why it works better than other offerings that might be cheaper or quicker.

People buy the impact of coaching. Even if they ask you what you do, don't spend time telling them the process you use.

Highlight the key points in these tips when describing the value you offer to potential clients and why having a coach, especially in turbulent, uncertain times, is the best way to accelerate growth.

- *Coaching activates the brain. Giving advice pacifies it*—When you tell people what to do, you activate their short-term memory in their thinking brain. If they don't act on your advice right away, your suggestion will get blocked by their worries and lost to the distractions that take up space in their brain soon after your conversation. And even if they think you have given them good information to support your recommendation, they may hesitate acting on it. Information doesn't change behavior. Do you *know* you should be doing something but you're not? Knowing doesn't translate into doing.

You can choose to scare people into changing, but then they learn for good "I have to do this as I was told before or else," so they resist changing what they do even when they can see good results when others apply new ways of thinking. If you want adaptable thinking and agile decision-making, don't scare them into learning.

In contrast to telling people what to do or trying to scare them into submission, coaching activates their thinking. Coaching pulls out the stories directing today's behavior so people can examine their thinking processes in a way they can't do for themselves. They then see the old beliefs that no longer serve them, consider the truth of a fear or doubt, discover gaps in their logic, identify needs that aren't being met, and recognize conflicts of values keeping them stuck. When they see new ways of approaching problems on their own, they act on their insights with more confidence even when there is uncertainty and risk.

■ *The smarter the person, the greater the need for coaching—* Smart people are the best rationalizers. They justify their thinking, decisions, and actions with little scrutiny, especially if challenged. They believe in the good reasons they present and will protect their opinions as facts.

Telling smart people they have to change is usually a waste of time. Reflecting their words and the emotions they express is the only way to get smart people to question their thoughts, shift their perspective, and try out new actions. Coaching makes them stop and think in a way they resist doing for themselves.

Even when someone thinks they know it all, coaching can open their mind to what else is possible.

■ *Coaching moves people through the discomfort of learning—* Being open to learning is not easy. Knowing is more comfortable than not knowing. Most people do not like the feelings of uncertainty, insecurity, and doubt that come with not knowing the answers. When you don't know what to do when faced with a difficult situation—or worse, how to explain what is going on—you feel unstable, even helpless. Stress fogs the brain when you feel out of control.

The brain likes to know what will happen next. It uses your past experiences to make sense of each moment. You depend on your brain to make the right decisions about your actions and engaging in typical interactions. Even when you sense what you are doing isn't in your best interest, you do what feels comfortable or familiar.

To open the window to see new ways of thinking, you must have someone who can summarize your thoughts and then ask questions you can't comfortably ask yourself. When you hear the words you speak and are asked about the emotions you express, your automatic processing is disrupted. You may feel sad, angry, or embarrassed when you finally see the holes in your logic, how your fears are limiting your choices, and how you allow what other people say you should do to control your actions. Your coach can help you process this information and form insights for moving forward. With active support over time, the new ways of thinking and behaving become the typical, and better, way of doing things.

When people stay stuck in their old stories, they live more in fear than fulfillment, creating conflicts and separation. Widespread use of a coaching approach in our conversations can uplift consciousness and healthy ways of living together in the world.

When Coaching Can
Make a Big Difference

Opportunities to coach people often show up in these scenarios, including both personal and work circumstances:

- Exploring ways to improve communications
- Facing fears of conflict and taking risks
- Finding solutions for dealing with difficult people and situations
- Igniting new ideas and innovative approaches
- Strengthening relationships at work and home
- Articulating desires and visions, both personally and professionally
- Managing stress and well-being to maximize energy
- Sorting through difficult decisions
- Experiencing greater fulfillment and success
- Dealing with work and life challenges
- Inspiring greater team performance
- Shifting the corporate culture
- Identifying development paths, both preparing for and succeeding in new roles
- Exploring the next chapter in life or the legacy a person wants to leave behind

Having Effective Discovery Conversations

Even before you explain how coaching works, if you can uncover a challenge the person is facing, you can tie the value of coaching to helping them resolve or dissolve the challenge. Here are some questions you can use to hear the specific pain points the person wants to relieve and uncover a coaching opportunity:

1. What is a challenge or nagging question you face right now in your life or work that you know you need to address but haven't?
2. If you have tried to address your challenge, what hasn't been as effective as you had hoped?
3. Do you know the cost of not addressing this situation now or in the future?
4. What could you gain if you could resolve this challenge or find a new way to live with it?
5. Are you interested in hearing how coaching might help you move forward?

If the answer to question 5 is yes, give them a taste of coaching so they recognize something they had not seen or wanted to consider up until now, and then they commit to taking at least one step forward.

APPENDIX A

Archetype Descriptions

The following is a list of archetype descriptions to help discover your selves concept:

- *The Wanderer* seeks new opportunities and freedom. You get bored easily, which leads you on a continual search for what's next. However, you can also lose your sense of self if constantly on the move.
- *The Pioneer* is also on the move but generally driven by one specific mission. You may become a Settler when you find a company or community that will allow you to realize your dreams.
- *The Queen or King* likes gathering people to complete a mission. You like to make decisions and are comfortable with the power you have for getting others to implement what you decide.
- *The Warrior* uses strength and intelligence to fight for making things better. You are ready to defend your ideas and vision at a moment's notice. When your passion turns to anger, you might overuse your Warrior strength and become a Bully who damages her relationships by forcing people to act and bluntly responding when they don't do as you command.

- *The Rebel* rejects both conformity and authority. Rebel energy is needed when traditional systems are strongly set in place and transformation is past due. The Rebel rises up even when rejecting authority and traditions is dangerous.

- *The Revolutionary* builds new structures based on a clear vision of what is possible (whereas Rebels break down old ones). However, if you do not earn the respect of your colleagues, you will be seen as a Rebel.

- *The Thinker* has learned to watch with keen eyes before speaking. You prepare your presentations carefully, knowing you are right about your conclusions. However, you are sensitive to criticism and tend to respond sarcastically or with quiet disdain.

- *The Scholar* has a strong academic background and draws on this knowledge to make theoretical arguments using research and strong examples. Like the Thinker, you defend your ideas more often than inviting debate. Practicing curiosity would improve relationships and growth.

- *The Adventurer* is an idea person. You love coming up with creative answers to problems. However, you are easily distracted, which can make it frustrating to work with you.

- *The Storyteller* loves to be the center of attention. You captivate your audiences with stories that help them learn. Sometimes your stories are irrelevant, making you look more out of touch than wise.

- *The Driver* is driven to achieve results. You accomplish a lot, but you can appear as a Taskmaster if you prioritize rules and goals over the needs of people. As a leader, Driver energy should be used only in emergencies.

- *The Steward* focuses on the needs and successes of others in service of the mission. When you help others to understand their talents, strengths, and dreams and then support them to use their gifts, you are a Steward leader.

- *The Visionary* uses stories and pictures to help others see possibilities beyond what is happening in the moment. If you also carry Adventurer energy, you will get bored easily with follow-up tasks. You may forget the details of your promises.

- *The Inspirer* prompts people into action by helping them feel they have the power to achieve significant results. You use active listening in addition to profound and encouraging language to rouse people into dedicated action.

- *The Hero* likes to lay out the plan and then courageously fight the battles to help smooth the way for change. Sometimes you fix too many problems on your own instead of engaging others to help.

- *The Collaborator* takes an active role in making sure all parties involved are fully participating. You take the time to listen and understand all points of view, which allows you to see the big-picture solutions. Some people will marvel at your patience. Others will see your actions as a waste of time, wishing you were more decisive.

- *The Martyr* works tirelessly to make changes and then expects to be recognized for the absolute dedication and personal sacrifices given. Contributions are significant, but the payment must be admiration to keep a positive attitude.

- *The Advocate* serves a cause that may be achieved or not. You know you don't have full control over the outcome, and the change might not be realized during your tenure in the role, but you fight for the cause anyway.

- *The Superstar* loves to be the head of the pack, outshining everyone in work and deeds. You become known for the outstanding quality of your work, which makes as many enemies as it does allies. This is a hard pattern to drop when moving into a leadership or collaborator role.

- *The Coach* trusts people are capable of finding their own way even when they aren't so sure of themselves. You become a thinking partner instead of a Teacher or Mentor, who provides solutions.

- *The Teacher* is an expert and possibly a lifelong learner with a mission to share the wisdom gathered. You may feel offended or rejected if your teaching is challenged or ignored.

- *The Healer* steps in to help people recover from being hurt. The healer can get caught up in saving or fixing people instead of just aiding them to mend and improve.

- *The Entertainer* loves to hold the attention of a group with something amusing or diverting. This can help when also being a Healer or Teacher when focused on healing or developing others. Entertainers can also be inspiring or amusing; your lightness lifts the energy and infuses hope.

- *The Mentor* is a wise and trusted sponsor or supporter. People seek your advice and insight. You are more inclined to share your wisdom than to draw it out of others.

- *The Mother or Father* serves to support, encourage, and protect those in their care. You do this from a position of power even if you show compassion.

- *The Nurturer* is a similar pattern offering encouragement and support but from a position of wanting to help or take care of others. If you sacrifice yourself in the process, you may slip into being a Martyr.

- *The Magician* likes making amazing results happen. Based on your many experiences, you can see through illusions and achieve grand things that others could not conceive. You believe that if one door closes, another one will soon open.

- *The Detective* has great powers of observation and sees details others often miss. You have a thirst for seeking the truth. Like the Coach, you are naturally curious, which makes you a good listener with solid intuition.

- *The Connector* weaves together the tasks of people from different perspectives and backgrounds to achieve a common goal. You may use many communication platforms to give people the opportunity to connect, including internet-based options.

- *The Fixer* loves to find answers and won't give up on a problem until the fix is found. You are as resourceful as you are persistent, but sometimes you need to know when it's time to move on.

- *The Companion* senses that a part of any life mission is to be in partnership with someone else. This can be a friend, spouse or domestic partner, or someone you are employed to assist.

- *The Idealist* is the perennial optimist who sees the glass half-full. You believe we construct our own realities, so why not create a good one? Without a clear vision, you might be seen as out of touch with reality and vulnerable to pitfalls.

- *The Artist* tends to be visual and uses creative skills to solve problems. You may, however, be temperamental when the value of your work is not acknowledged.

- *The Gambler* is a risk-taker. You trust your intuition, which can make it difficult for you to hear and accept other people's ideas. You leap when a good opportunity shows up, often without considering the risks.

Note: The first list of archetypes I developed can be found in my book *Wander Woman*.[1]

APPENDIX B

Values to Live By

Values are strongly held aspects of life that make you feel happy and secure in your relationships, home environment, and work. Your values may conflict with those you live and work with. It is important to determine when you feel you are living a life you are eager to wake up to. What contributes to your feelings of contentment, satisfaction, pride, and joy? To be happy, you must live in alignment with your values, not in resentment or regret for compromising what you hold dear. Sorting out the difference between *shoulds* (when other people tell you what decisions to make and how to live your life) and what is most important to you can often be difficult. Knowing your personal life values can give you the perspective and courage to make important decisions.

This list can help you sort out what is most important to you. See if you can choose your top five to six values that you most want to honor and live by.

Achievement—Successfully completing or contributing to visible tasks, goals, and projects.

Advancement—Getting ahead and aspiring to higher levels in career or personal development.

Adventure—Engaging in new experiences and discoveries that may involve risk and testing limits.

Aesthetics—Having the desire for beautiful surroundings, artistic expression, and sensory pleasure.

Assertiveness—Confidently speaking beliefs and setting personal boundaries.

Balance—Feeling stable and grounded.

Challenge—Testing and hopefully conquering what feels dangerous or difficult.

Community—Having neighbors, coworkers, or a society who help each other achieve common goals.

Competence—Being good at what you do, leading to feeling confident, capable, and effective.

Creativity—Finding new ways to do things, composing, and discovering what was not seen before.

Courage—Bravely standing up for self or others even when doing so might be uncomfortable, risky, or painful.

Environment—Respecting the earth and living in safe, comfortable spaces.

Ethics—Honoring practices and principles that govern behavior.

Fairness—Respecting everyone's rights and removing prejudice and favoritism in words and actions.

Family—Taking care of and spending time with relatives and other people you feel close to.

Freedom—Ability to make one's own decisions and choices.

Friendship—Having close companionship and ongoing and supportive relationships.

Fun—Loving to do what brings amusement, pleasure, and joy.

Happiness—Feeling joyful, content, or purposely fulfilled.

Health—Maintaining and enhancing physical well-being.

Helping—Taking care of others and assisting others to flourish.

Honesty—Being sincere and truthful and keeping promises.

Inclusion—Welcoming everyone to participate and making them feel they equally belong.

Independence—Being self-reliant or having autonomy when living and working with others.

Inner harmony—Being free from inner conflict and feeling integrated, whole, and tranquil.

Integrity—Acting in line with beliefs and doing what you said you would.

Intimacy—Having deep connections with others.

Kindness—Acting thoughtfully with consideration for other's feelings.

Learning—Deepening knowledge and expanding perspective for personal growth.

Loyalty—Acting with devotion to people, groups, or a cause.

Patience—Calmly accepting delays and a slow pace.

Peace—Living in harmony with people, groups, and the environment.

Perseverance—Pushing through to the end; completing tasks and goals even when difficult.

Personal growth—Continually developing and improving one's self.

Power—Having the authority or ability to direct events or people or make things happen.

Practicality—Acting with logic, evidence, or good sense when making decisions.

Prosperity—Flourishing, easily obtaining desires, or feeling wealthy or satisfied.

Religion—Experiencing a deep connection with one's faith.

Security—Being free from worry and being safe from threats.

Simplicity—Having an uncluttered environment, enjoying natural states, and communicating easily.

Spirituality—Believing in the divine and an unseen power or living with gratitude and appreciation.

Social justice—Working to establish fairness in society, righting what is wrong and not equal.

Stability—Having a sense of certainty and predictability and adhering to structure and systems.

Status—Being highly regarded in one's social group.

Teamwork—Cooperating with others toward a common goal and collaborating to produce a result.

Tradition—Respecting the way things have been done in the past; honoring rituals and heritage.

Winning—Success when competing and coming out on top.

Notes

Introduction

1. Carin Eriksson Lindvall, "Renewal by Subtraction," *Psychology Today*, November/December 2021, 60.

2. Dan McAdams, "The Stories We Tell about Ourselves: Understanding Our Personal Narratives," interview by Antonia Mufarech, North by Northwestern, January 25, 2022, northbynorthwestern.com/the-stories -we-tell-about-ourselves/.

3. Mark Leary, "The Case for Being Skeptical of Yourself," *Psychology Today*, November/December 2021, 41–42.

4. Michael Gazzaniga, *Who's in Charge?: Free Will and the Science of the Brain* (NY: Ecco, 2011), 43.

5. John Dewey, *How We Think* (Boston: D. C. Heath, 1909), 18.

Part 1

1. David Dunning et al., "Trust at Zero Acquaintance: More a Matter of Respect Than Expectation of Reward," *Journal of Personality and Social Psychology* 107, no. 1 (July 2014): 122–141, doi.org/10.1037/a0036673.

Chapter 1

1. Kenneth Nowack, "Facilitating Successful Behavior Change: Beyond Goal Setting to Goal Flourishing," *Consulting Psychology Journal: Practice and Research* 69, no. 3 (2017): 153–171.

2. Simon Weil, *Waiting for God* (NY: Routledge, 2021), 67.

3. Iris Murdoch, *The Sovereignty of Good* (London: Routledge Classics, 2001), 82.

Chapter 2

1. Amy C. Edmondson, "Managing the Risk of Learning: Psychological Safety in Work Teams," in *International Handbook of Organizational Teamwork*, ed. Michael A. West et al. (Hoboken, NJ: John Wiley, 2003), 255–275.

2. Shari M. Geller and Stephen W. Porges, "Therapeutic Presence: Neurophysiological Mechanisms Mediating Feeling Safe in Therapeutic Relationships," *Journal of Psychotherapy Integration* 24, no. 3 (2014): 178–192.

3. Kate Thieda, "Brené Brown on Empathy vs. Sympathy," *Psychology Today*, August 12, 2014, psychologytoday.com/us/blog/partnering -in-mental-health/201408/bren-brown-empathy-vs-sympathy-0.

4. Carmen Nobel, "Is Your iPhone Turning You into a Wimp?" Harvard Business School Working Knowledge (blog), June 24, 2013, hbswk.hbs.edu /item/is-your-iphone-turning-you-into-a-wimp.

5. Merriam-Webster, "What's the Difference between 'Sympathy' and 'Empathy'?," accessed May 7, 2023, merriam-webster.com/words-at-play /sympathy-empathy-difference.

Chapter 3

1. Saundra Dalton-Smith, *Sacred Rest: Recover Your Life, Renew Your Energy, Restore Your Sanity* (NY: Hachette, 2019).

Chapter 4

1. Steven Rose, *The Future of the Brain: The Promise and Perils of Tomorrow's Neuroscience* (NY: Oxford University, 2005) 103, 166–167.

2. Pico Iyer, "The Beauty of What We'll Never Know," TED Summit, October 2016, Vancouver, BC, video, 9:57, ted.com/talks/pico_iyer _the_beauty_of_what_we_ll_never_know/.

3. Shaun Gallagher et al. ed., *A Neurophenomenology of Awe and Wonder: Towards a Non-reductionist Cognitive Science* (London: Palgrave Macmillan, 2015), 22–23.

Part 2

1. Ephrat Livni, "It's Better to Understand Something Than to Know It," Quartz, November 14, 2017, qz.com/1123896/its-better-to-understand -something-than-to-know-it.

Chapter 5

1. John Dewey, *How We Think* (Boston: D. C. Heath, 1910), 11.
2. Rutger Bregman, *Humankind: A Hopeful History* (NY: Little, Brown, 2020), 23.
3. Gorka Bartolomé et al., "Right Cortical Activations during Generation of Creative Insights: An Electroencephalographic Study of Coaching," *Frontiers in Education* 7 (April 25, 2022).

Chapter 6

1. Anne Lamott, *Bird by Bird: Some Instructions on Writing and Life* (NY: Anchor Books, 1995).
2. Stuart Semple, "David Bowie on Why You Should Never Play to the Gallery," YouTube, 1:00, youtube.com/watch?v=cNbnef_eXBM&t=4s.
3. Julian Treasure, *How to Be Heard: Secrets for Powerful Speaking and Listening* (Coral Gables, FL: Mango, 2017), 151–157.

Chapter 8

1. Tori Rodriguez, "Taking the Bad with the Good," *Scientific American Mind* 24, no. 2 (April 2013): 26–27.
2. Nessa Bryce, "The Aha! Moment," *Scientific American Mind* 23, no. 5s, (January 2015): 48–53.
3. Shelley Carson, "The Unleashed Mind: Why Creative People Are Eccentric," *Scientific American Mind*, May 1, 2011, scientificamerican.com /article/the-unleashed-mind/.
4. John Kounios and Mark Beeman, "The Cognitive Neuroscience of Insight," *Annual Review of Psychology* 65, no. 1 (January 2014): 71–93.
5. Gordon Hempton and John Grossman, *One Square Inch of Silence* (NY: Free Press, 2009), 2.Part 3

Part 3

1. Robert Biswas-Diener, *Positive Provocation: 25 Questions to Elevate Your Coaching Practice* (Oakland: Berrett-Koehler, 2023), xvii.

Chapter 10

1. Parker Palmer, *On the Brink of Everything: Grace, Gravity, and Getting Older* (Oakland: Berrett-Koehler Publishers, 2018), 174.

Chapter 12

1. Terry R. Bacon, *Measuring the Effectiveness of Executive Coaching* (Korn/Ferry Institute, January 2011), issuu.com/kornferryinternational /docs/__measuring_the_effectiveness_of_executive_coachin.

Chapter 14

1. Shoba Sreenivasan and Linda E. Weinberger, "The Need for Social Approval," *Psychology Today*, June 15, 2020, psychologytoday.com/intl /blog/emotional-nourishment/202006/the-need-social-approval.

Chapter 15

1. Jim Taylor, "Personal Growth: Your Values, Your Life," *Psychology Today*, May 7, 2012, psychologytoday.com/us/blog/the-power-prime /201205/personal-growth-your-values-your-life.

2. Maria Popova, "Escaping the Trap of Efficiency: The Counterintuitive Antidote to the Time-Anxiety That Haunts and Hampers Our Search for Meaning," Marginalian (blog), themarginalian.org/2021/12/20/four -thousand-weeks-oliver-burkeman/.

3. PEAK Values Card Deck, PEAK Fleet, 2020, thepeakfleet.com /product/peak-values-core-values-card-deck/.

Part 5

1. Sara Canaday, *Coaching Essentials for Manager: The Tools You Need to Ignite Greatness in Each Employee* (NY: McGraw Hill Education, 2023), 59.

Chapter 16

1. Valeria Sabater, "Thinking Aloud Improves Mental Ability," Exploring Your Mind, November 15, 2021, exploringyourmind.com /thinking-aloud-improves-mental-ability/.

Appendix A

1. Marcia Reynolds, *Wander Woman: How High-Achieving Women Find Contentment and Direction* (San Francisco: Berrett-Koehler, 2010), 52–60.

Index

About the Author

Dr. **Marcia Reynolds**, president of Covisioning LLC, is passionate about researching, writing about, and teaching people around the world how to engage in powerful conversations that activate positive change. From government agencies and large multinational companies to coaching programs in Asia, the Middle East, Europe, and the Americas, she is constantly invited to present on fresh new ways to move forward on the path of coaching mastery.

Marcia is a pioneer in the coaching profession. She was the fifth global president of the International Coaching Federation and inducted into its Circle of Distinction for her years of service to the global coaching community. She is recognized by Global Gurus as one of the top five coaches in the world and is the creator of the renowned Coaching.com program Breakthrough Coaching.

Before she launched her own business, her greatest success came from designing the employee development program for a global semiconductor company facing bankruptcy. Within three years, the company became the number one stock market success in 1993. She attributes the success to improving communications and establishing the foundation for building a coaching culture.

Interviews and excerpts from her books *Coach the Person, Not the Problem*; *The Discomfort Zone: How Leaders Turn Difficult Conversations into Breakthroughs*; *Outsmart Your Brain*; and *Wander Woman: How High Achieving Women Find Contentment and Direction* have appeared in many places, including *Fast Company*, Forbes.com, CNN.com, *Psychology Today*, the *Globe and Mail*, and the *Wall Street Journal*, and she has appeared in business magazines in Europe and Asia and on *ABC World News*.

Marcia's favorite pastimes are hiking and learning. She holds a doctorate in organizational psychology and two master's degrees in learning psychology and communications.

Marcia is passionate about coaching; email her if you have a need or dream where coaching can help at Marcia@covisioning.com. Her website is covisioning.com.

Berrett–Koehler
BK Publishers

Berrett-Koehler is an independent publisher dedicated to an ambitious mission: *Connecting people and ideas to create a world that works for all.*

Our publications span many formats, including print, digital, audio, and video. We also offer online resources, training, and gatherings. And we will continue expanding our products and services to advance our mission.

We believe that the solutions to the world's problems will come from all of us, working at all levels: in our society, in our organizations, and in our own lives. Our publications and resources offer pathways to creating a more just, equitable, and sustainable society. They help people make their organizations more humane, democratic, diverse, and effective (and we don't think there's any contradiction there). And they guide people in creating positive change in their own lives and aligning their personal practices with their aspirations for a better world.

And we strive to practice what we preach through what we call "The BK Way." At the core of this approach is *stewardship,* a deep sense of responsibility to administer the company for the benefit of all of our stakeholder groups, including authors, customers, employees, investors, service providers, sales partners, and the communities and environment around us. Everything we do is built around stewardship and our other core values of *quality, partnership, inclusion,* and *sustainability.*

This is why Berrett-Koehler is the first book publishing company to be both a B Corporation (a rigorous certification) and a benefit corporation (a for-profit legal status), which together require us to adhere to the highest standards for corporate, social, and environmental performance. And it is why we have instituted many pioneering practices (which you can learn about at www.bkconnection.com), including the Berrett-Koehler Constitution, the Bill of Rights and Responsibilities for BK Authors, and our unique Author Days.

We are grateful to our readers, authors, and other friends who are supporting our mission. We ask you to share with us examples of how BK publications and resources are making a difference in your lives, organizations, and communities at www.bkconnection.com/impact.

Dear reader,

Thank you for picking up this book and welcome to the worldwide BK community! You're joining a special group of people who have come together to create positive change in their lives, organizations, and communities.

What's BK all about?

Our mission is to connect people and ideas to create a world that works for all.

Why? Our communities, organizations, and lives get bogged down by old paradigms of self-interest, exclusion, hierarchy, and privilege. But we believe that can change. That's why we seek the leading experts on these challenges—and share their actionable ideas with you.

A welcome gift

To help you get started, we'd like to offer you a **free copy** of one of our bestselling ebooks:

www.bkconnection.com/welcome

When you claim your **free ebook**, you'll also be subscribed to our blog.

Our freshest insights

Access the best new tools and ideas for leaders at all levels on our blog at ideas.bkconnection.com.

Sincerely,

Your friends at Berrett-Koehler

Certified

Corporation

MIX
Paper from
responsible sources
FSC® C016245